THE
ELEMENTS OF STYLE

By William Strunk Jr.

CLASSIC EDITION
2018 UPDATE

Richard De A'Morelli, Editor

SPECTRUM INK PUBLISHING

The Elements of Style: Classic Edition (2018)

ISBN numbers:

978-1-64399-000-2	Paperback
978-1-64399-001-9	Mobi / Kindle
978-1-64399-002-6	EPUB
978-1-64399-003-3	Paperback (Ingram)
978-1-64399-004-0	Hardcover

Spectrum Ink Canada
Vancouver, British Columbia

Spectrum Ink USA
San Luis Obispo, California

Website:
http://spectrum.org/books

Table of Contents

Preface

The Elements of Style was written in 1918 by William Strunk Jr., an English professor at Cornell University. He distributed it as a handout listing basic grammar tips for students in his English classes, and he probably never imagined that it still would be widely read a century later. Strunk's legacy endured, and his book has helped generations of college students and writers learn the basics of English grammar. *Elements of* Style was recognized as "one of the 100 most influential books written in English" by *Time* in 2011; and author Stephen King recommended it as must reading for all aspiring writers.

In a preface to the first edition, Strunk wrote: "This book aims to describe in just a few pages the principal requirements of plain English style. Its goal is to lighten the task of instructors and students by concentrating on a few essentials, the rules of usage, and principles of composition most commonly violated. To fulfill these criteria, the book will describe three rules for the use of the comma, rather than a dozen or more, and one for the use of the semicolon, in the belief that these four rules will provide for most of the punctuation that is required by nineteen sentences out of twenty. Likewise, the book discusses only those principles pertaining to the paragraph and the sentence of the widest application. Thus, we will endeavor to cover only a small portion of the field of English grammar and style."

This *Classic Edition* is a centennial tribute to Strunk's book, which is not only a useful grammar primer but a nostalgic link to a fabled time in American history that brought the Art Deco era and the Roaring Twenties. Many of the grammar rules in these pages are as valid today as they were a century ago; but, the world has changed, and the English language has changed with it, making some of Strunk's rules obsolete. This edition contains the full text of *The Elements of Style*, plus numerous enhancements not found in other public domain versions of Strunk's book, including:

1. Editor's notes have been inserted throughout the book to flag grammar rules now considered obsolete, and to provide up-to-date usage rules for students and writers.

2. Emojis have been added to most examples to help readers easily identify correctly written passages from errors.

3. A Study Guide is included in the last chapter.

4. The paperback version includes blank, lined pages at the back of the book for convenient notetaking.

5. The e-book version has been restyled for improved display on the latest generations of digital reader devices.

In addition, this 2018 Update contains an expanded Introduction and two new chapters: *Basic Rules of Capitalization* (Chapter 3) presents an in-depth list of capitalization rules that confuse many writers; and, *Style Rules for Better Writing* (Chapter 7) offers a collection of tips on how to improve your writing, as well as grammar and style mistakes to avoid when revising and self-editing your work.

Prof. Strunk's book stresses the importance of writing clear and grammatically correct prose. It is a blueprint that students and writers can follow to write their thoughts and ideas in a crisp, concise, and effective manner. The clearer your writing, the more likely it is that readers will grasp the points you are trying to make.

If you need a more comprehensive handbook on grammar and style, you may find *Elements of Style 2017* useful. Intended for college students, writers, editors, and anyone else who is called upon to write grammar-perfect final drafts, this handy guide builds on Strunk's fundamental rules and includes more than 500 grammar and style rules from authoritative sources. *Elements of Style 2017* is available in e-book and paperback editions at your favorite bookstore or it can be purchased online at: https://amazon.com/dp/B01MD0396I

Now, let's begin reading Strunk's *Elements of Style* and take the first step toward correct and effective writing.

Foreword

Why English Grammar Matters

By Joseph Devlin, M.A.

To write correctly and effectively, the fundamental principles of English grammar must be mastered. No matter how badly you want to write, no matter how deep your feelings, and no matter how exciting the ideas you want to share with others, if you don't know the basic rules of how to correctly form sentences and the relation of words to one another, your writing will lack coherency. Imagine for a moment a novel with a sensational idea, unforgettable characters, set in an exotic place, and chock full of suspense—no matter how great the idea might be, if the story is penned by a writer who lacks a basic grasp of the English language, the result will be poorly written.

Learning how to write correctly should be an easy challenge considering that the average person's vocabulary consists of a mere 2,000 words. Knowing the definitions of those words and knowing how to put them together in a sentence won't make you a master of the English language, but it will make you a competent writer, and most people who read what you write will understand it. You might think 2,000 words is a small number, considering how many thousands of words are in the dictionary. But nobody ever uses all the words in the dictionary, and there is really no need to use them. If no one understands the words you use in your writing, you will have no audience; and if you have no readers, you will have no reason to write.

The English language contains at least 250,000 distinct words. Knowing just one percent of these words will suffice for nearly every writing endeavor you might wish to undertake. Shakespeare's classic works contain 15,000 different words, but more than 10,000 are obsolete today. Of course, you might want to expand your vocabulary and use interesting words for the sake of variety or to impress your reader; or maybe a common word just doesn't have the right ring to it. Maybe you don't want to refer to a spade as simply a spade—you'd rather call it a spatulous device for abrading the surface of the soil. The problem is, most of your readers won't have any idea what you are talking about. So, it's better to stick with familiar words that are widely used and understood. Proper grammatical structure of the several thousand English words you will likely use can be learned with relative ease.

Rules of grammar are necessary and should be followed so that you can express thoughts and ideas in a clear and effective manner. Written correctly, your words will convey a definite meaning and have impact on your readers. But hard and fast rules cannot make a writer. If you have no ideas to put into words, no thought can be expressed, and no writing can take place. You must have distinct thoughts and ideas before you can express them in written form.

The best way to learn to write is to sit down and write, just as the best way to learn to ride a bicycle is to mount the wheel and work the pedals. Write first about common things and familiar subjects. Familiar themes are always the best for the beginner. Don't attempt to describe a scene in Australia if you have never been there and know nothing of the country. Never struggle to find subjects—thousands exist around you. Describe what you saw yesterday: a fire, a crowded store, a fight on the street, an exquisite sunset, and be original in your description. Imitate the best writers in their style, but not in their exact words. Get off the beaten path and make a pathway of your own.

The Nine Parts of Speech

To grasp the basic rules of grammar and the proper placement of words in sentences, it's important to know that all words in the English language fall into nine categories, called "the parts of speech." They are: noun, article, pronoun, adjective, verb, adverb, preposition, conjunction, and interjection.

The **noun** is the most important of the nine parts of speech, as all the rest are more or less dependent upon it. A noun refers to the name of any person, place, or thing, which includes tangible objects and abstract concepts. Nouns fall into two categories: proper and common. Proper nouns are formal names, as the names of people (John, Mary, Bob); places (London, Paris, Seattle); and countries (Canada, England). Common nouns refer to everything else in more general terms (man, city, nation).

An **article** is a word placed before a noun to show whether the noun is used in a particular or general sense. English has two articles: *a* (or *an*) and *the*. The former is called the "indefinite" article because it does not refer to a particular person or thing but indicates the noun in its most general sense; for instance, *a man* can mean any man on the planet. The latter is called the "definite" article because it refers to a specific person or thing; thus, *the man* means a specific individual.

An **adjective** is a word that qualifies a noun, meaning it shows or points out some distinguishing mark or feature of the noun. For example: a *black* dog, a *pretty* woman, a *cold* wind.

A **pronoun** is a word used in place of a noun so that you don't have to repeat the same noun too often and fall into tedious repetition. Consider the following sentence:

☺ John gave his pen to James, and then he lent it to Jane to write her copy with it.

Without pronouns, we would have to write this sentence as:

✗ John gave John's pen to James, and then James lent the pen to Jane to write Jane's copy with the pen.

Pronouns fall into two categories: singular and plural. The singular pronouns are: *I, me, my, mine; you, your, yours; he, him, his; she, her, hers;* and *it, its;* and the plural are: *we, us, our, ours; you, your, yours;* and *they, them, their, theirs.*

A **verb** is a word that signifies action or the doing of something; or it may be a word that affirms, commands, or asks a question. The phrase *John the table* contains no assertion and thus no verb. But when the word *strikes* is introduced, something is affirmed—*strikes* is a verb and completes the thought, giving meaning to the group.

An **adverb** is a word that modifies a verb, an adjective, or another adverb. In the following examples, the adverbs are underlined. In the first example, the adverb shows the manner in which the writing is done. In the second, the adverb modifies the adjective *diligent.* In the third, the adverb modifies the adjective *beautiful.*

He writes <u>well</u>.

He is <u>remarkably</u> diligent.

She is <u>very</u> beautiful

Note that adverbs are mainly used to express in one word what would otherwise require two or more words.

A **preposition** connects words, clauses, and sentences together and shows the relation between them, as:

My hand is on the table.

This sentence shows relation between *hand* and *table,* and the preposition *on* connects the two words. Prepositions are usually placed before the words whose connection or relation with other words they point out.

A **conjunction** is a word that joins words, phrases, clauses, and sentences together. For instance, the conjunctions are underlined in these examples:

John and James.

My father and mother arrived, but I did not see them.

I prefer apples or strawberries, and Tyrone prefers oranges.

The most common conjunctions are: *and, also; either, or; neither, nor; though, yet; but, however; for, that; because, since; therefore, wherefore, then,* and *if.*

An **interjection** is a word that expresses surprise, shock, or some other sudden emotion. In the passage below, *Ah!* expresses surprise, and *alas* expresses distress.

Ah! There he comes; alas! what shall I do?

Nouns, adjectives, verbs, and adverbs become interjections when they are uttered as one-word exclamations: *Fire! Nonsense! Strange! No!*

Three Essentials of Effective Writing

The three essentials of effective writing in the English language are: purity, perspicuity, and precision. *Purity* refers to the use of proper English. It means writing without the use of slang words and expletives (except when writing fiction and then used sparingly or as appropriate for a certain audience), obsolete terms, foreign idioms, ambiguous expressions, and grammatically incorrect language.

Perspicuity denotes clear expression of thoughts conveyed in unequivocal language, so there is no misunderstanding of the thought or idea that the writer wishes to express. Ambiguous words, words of double meaning, and words that might be construed in a sense different from that intended should be avoided. Perspicuity requires a style that is clear and concise.

Precision requires concise and exact expression, free from redundancy—a style that is clear and simple enough so that the reader can immediately comprehend the meaning of the writer's words. Long and involved sentences are avoided, as well as sentences that are too short and abrupt. Its object is to strike the golden mean in such a way as to rivet the attention of the reader on the words you have written.

George Orwell's Advice to Writers

Author George Orwell offered some poignant advice on grammar and style to writers in his discourse on *Politics and the English Language*. These suggestions are worth remembering and should be followed if you want to see an improvement in the clarity and quality of your writing.

—Never use a long word where a short one will do.

—If it is possible to cut a word out, always cut it out.

—Never use the passive where you can use the active.

—Never use a foreign phrase, a scientific word, or jargon if you can think of an everyday English equivalent to use instead.

—A scrupulous writer, in every sentence that he writes, will ask himself at least four questions: 1. What am I trying to say? 2. What words will express it? 3. What image or idiom will make it clearer? 4. Is this image fresh enough to have an effect?

A Writer's Recipe for Success

As you go forward in your endeavors, possess the ambition to succeed as a writer, and you will succeed. Remove the word "failure" from your lexicon. Do not acknowledge it. Let every obstacle you encounter be but a stepping stone in the path of progress towards the goal of mastering the fundamentals of English grammar so that you can write correctly and effectively.

Chapter 1

ELEMENTARY RULES OF USAGE

I t has been observed that the best writers sometimes disregard the rules of rhetoric. When they do so, however, readers will usually find in the sentence some compensating merit to counterbalance the violation. Unless a writer is certain that he will provide the same benefit, he will do best to follow the rules. After the writer has learned, by studying and adhering to the rules, to write plain English adequate for everyday use, let him look for the secrets of style in studying the masters of literature.

Rule 1. Form the possessive singular of nouns by adding 's.

Follow this rule regardless of the final consonant. These usages are correct:

> Charles's friend
>
> Burns's poems
>
> the witch's malice

This is the rule followed by the U.S. Government Printing Office and the Oxford University Press. Exceptions are the possessive of ancient proper names ending in -es and -is; the possessive *Jesus';* and such forms as *for conscience' sake, for righteousness' sake.* But such forms as *Achilles' heel, Moses' laws,* and *Isis' temple* are commonly rewritten as:

> the heel of Achilles
>
> the laws of Moses
>
> the temple of Isis

Do not use an apostrophe with the pronominal posses-
sives *hers, its, theirs, yours,* and *oneself.*

**Rule 2. In a series of three or more terms with a single
conjunction, use a comma after each term except the
last.**

For example:

> red, white, and blue

> gold, silver, or copper

> He opened the letter, read it, and made a note of its
> contents.

This is consistent with the guidelines of the Government
Printing Office and of the Oxford University Press.

➡ *Editor's Note:* A comma placed before a conjunction in a
series of three or more terms is called a serial comma or an
Oxford comma. Depending on the style guide you are using,
such commas may be deemed either required or incorrect in
modern writing. For example, *Chicago Manual of Style* states
that serial commas should be used, while *Associated Press
Stylebook* advises against them.

In the names of business firms omit the last comma, as,

> Brown, Shipley & Co.

**Rule 3. Enclose parenthetic expressions between
commas.**

A parenthetic expression is a clause or phrase that is inserted
within another clause or phrase. In a sense, it interrupts the
flow of the first expression; usually, it can be omitted and you
will still have a complete sentence, as,

> The best way to see a country, unless you are pressed
> for time, is to travel on foot.

This rule is difficult to apply, as it is often hard to decide whether a single word, such as *however*, or a brief phrase, is or is not parenthetic. If the interruption to the flow of the sentence is but slight, the writer may safely omit the commas. But whether the interruption be slight or considerable, one comma must be never inserted and the other omitted. In the following examples where a single comma is used, none of the expressions are correct:

> ✗ Marjorie's husband, Colonel Nelson paid us a visit yesterday.

> ☺ Marjorie's husband, Colonel Nelson, paid us a visit yesterday.

> ✗ My brother you will be pleased to hear, is now in perfect health.

> ☺ My brother, you will be pleased to hear, is now in perfect health.

If a parenthetic expression is preceded by a conjunction, write the first comma before the conjunction, not after it.

> ☺ He saw us coming, and unaware that we had learned of his treachery, greeted us with a smile.

The following constructions should always be regarded as parenthetic expressions and should be enclosed between commas (or, at the end of the sentence, between a comma and a period):

> 1. The year, when forming part of a date, and the day of the month, when following the day of the week, as:

> February to July, 1916

> April 6, 1917

> Monday, November 11, 1918

> 2. The abbreviations *etc.* and *Jr.*

3. Non-restrictive relative clauses, meaning those that do not serve to identify or define the antecedent noun, and similar clauses introduced by conjunctions indicating time or place.

In the following sentence, the clause introduced by *which* does not clearly identify which of several possible audiences is being referenced; what audience is in question is supposed to be already known. The clause adds, parenthetically, a statement supplementing that in the main clause. The sentence is a combination of two statements which could have been written independently, as in the second example:

✗ The audience, which had at first been indifferent, became more and more interested.

☺ The audience had at first been indifferent. It became more and more interested.

Compare the restrictive relative clause, not set off by commas, in this sentence:

☺ The candidate who best meets these requirements will be hired for the job.

Here the clause introduced by *who* does serve to tell which of several possible candidates is meant; the sentence cannot be split up into two independent statements.

The difference in punctuation in the two sentences below is based on the same principle:

Nether Stowey, where Coleridge wrote *The Rime of the Ancient Mariner*, is just a few miles from Bridgewater.

The day will come when you'll admit your mistake.

Nether Stowey is completely identified by its name; the statement about Coleridge is therefore supplementary and parenthetic. The *day* spoken of is identified only by the dependent clause, which is therefore restrictive.

Similar in principle to the enclosing of parenthetic expressions between commas is the setting off by commas of phrases or dependent clauses preceding or following the main clause of a sentence. For example:

> Partly by hard fighting, partly by diplomatic skill, they enlarged their dominions to the east, and rose to royal rank with the possession of Sicily, exchanged afterwards for Sardinia.

Other illustrations may be found in examples provided under Rules 4, 5, 6, 7, 16 and 18 below.

Be careful that you do not set off independent clauses by commas. See Rule 5 for clarification and examples.

Rule 4. Place a comma before a conjunction introducing a coordinate clause.

> ✗ The early records of the city have disappeared, and the story of its first years can no longer be reconstructed.

> ✗ The situation is perilous, but there is still one chance of escape.

Sentences of this type, isolated from their context, may seem to be in need of rewriting. They make sense when we reach the comma, and the second clause has the appearance of an afterthought. Further, the conjunction *and* is the least specific of connectives. Used between independent clauses, it indicates only that a relation exists between them without defining that relation. In the example above, the relation is that of cause and result. The two sentences might be rewritten:

> ☺ As the early records of the city have disappeared, the story of its first years cannot be reconstructed.

> ☺ Although the situation is perilous, there is still one chance of escape.

Or the subordinate clauses might be replaced by phrases:

☺ Owing to the disappearance of the early records of the city, the story of its first years can no longer be reconstructed.

☺ In this perilous situation, there is still one chance of escape.

It is not necessarily good style to make all of your sentences too uniformly compact and periodic. An occasional loose sentence prevents the style from becoming too formal and gives the reader a bit of relief. Consequently, loose sentences of the type first quoted are common in casual, non-technical writing. But be careful not to construct too many of your sentences after this pattern (see Rule 14).

Two-part sentences of which the second member is introduced by *as* (in the sense of *because*), *for*, *or*, *nor*, and *while* (in the sense of *and at the same time*) likewise require a comma before the conjunction.

If the second member is introduced by an adverb, a semicolon rather than a comma is required (see Rule 5). The connectives *so* and *yet* may be used either as adverbs or as conjunctions, accordingly as the second clause is felt to be coordinate or subordinate; so either punctuation mark may be appropriate. Note, however, that these uses of *so* (equivalent to *accordingly* or to *so that*) are somewhat colloquial and should, as a rule, be avoided in writing. A simple correction that usually works is to omit the word *so* and begin the first clause with *as* or *since*:

☺ As I had never been in the place before, I had difficulty in finding my way about.

The above construction is preferable to:

✗ I had never been in the place before; so I had difficulty in finding my way about.

If a dependent clause, or an introductory phrase that must be set off by a comma, precedes the second independent clause, no comma is needed after the conjunction.

☺ The situation is perilous, but if we are prepared to act promptly, there is still one chance of escape.

When the subject is the same for both clauses and is expressed only once, a comma is required if the connective is *but*. If the connective is *and*, omit the comma if the relation between the two statements is close or immediate.

☺ I have heard his arguments, but am still unconvinced.

☺ He has had several years' experience and is thoroughly competent.

Rule 5. Do not join independent clauses by a comma.

If two or more clauses, grammatically complete and not joined by a conjunction, are written to form a compound sentence, the proper punctuation mark is a semicolon.

☺ Stevenson's romances are entertaining; they are full of exciting adventures.

☺ It is nearly half past five; we cannot reach town before dark.

It is equally correct to write the above as two sentences each and replace the semicolons by periods.

☺ Stevenson's romances are entertaining. They are full of exciting adventures.

☺ It is nearly half past five. We cannot reach town before dark.

If a conjunction is inserted, the proper mark is a comma (Rule 4).

☺ Stevenson's romances are entertaining, for they are full of exciting adventures.

☺ It is nearly half past five, and we cannot reach town before dark.

A comparison of the three forms given above will show clearly that the first is preferable. It is, at least in the examples given, better than the second form, because it suggests a close relationship between the two statements in a way that the second does not attempt. It is better than the third, because it is briefer and therefore more direct and concise. Indeed, this simple method of indicating relationship between statements is one of the most useful devices of composition. The relationship, as in the above examples, is commonly one of cause or of consequence.

Note that if the second clause is preceded by an adverb, such as *accordingly, besides, then, therefore,* or *thus,* and not by a conjunction, the semicolon is still required.

But note two exceptions to this rule. First, if the clauses are very short and are alike in form, a comma is usually acceptable:

☺ Man proposes, God disposes.

☺ The gate swung apart, the bridge fell, the portcullis was drawn up.

In these examples the relation is not one of cause or consequence. Also in the colloquial form of expression, as the following, a comma, not a semicolon, is required:

☺ I hardly knew him, he was so changed.

However, this form of expression is not appropriate in writing, except in the dialogue of a story or play, or perhaps in a familiar letter or other casual writing.

Rule 6. Do not break sentences in two.

In other words, do not use periods for commas. While it is acceptable to break a compound sentence into two shorter elements, where both form complete sentences, doing so often results in choppy wording. Especially avoid breaking sentences in two when one part or the other does not form a complete sentence, as,

> ✗ I met them on a Cunard liner several years ago. Coming home from Liverpool to New York.

> ✗ He was an interesting talker. A man who had traveled the world and lived in a dozen countries.

In both these examples, the first period should be replaced by a comma, and the next word written with a lowercase letter.

It is permissible to make an emphatic word or expression serve the purpose of a sentence and to punctuate it accordingly:

> ☺ Again and again he called out. No reply.

You must be certain, however, that the emphasis is warranted, and that you will not be suspected of a mere blunder in syntax or in punctuation.

Rules 3, 4 5, and 6 cover the most important principles in punctuating ordinary sentences; they should be so thoroughly mastered that their application becomes second nature.

Rule 7. A participial phrase at the beginning of a sentence must refer to the grammatical subject.

> Walking slowly down the road, he saw a woman accompanied by two children.

The word *walking* refers to the subject of the sentence, not to the woman. If you want to make it refer to the woman, you must recast the sentence:

He saw a woman accompanied by two children, walking slowly down the road.

Participial phrases preceded by a conjunction or preposition, nouns in apposition, adjectives, and adjective phrases come under the same rule if they begin the sentence.

X On arriving in Chicago, his friends met him at the station.

☺ When he arrived (or, On his arrival) in Chicago, his friends met him at the station.

X A soldier of proved valor, they entrusted him with the defense of the city.

☺ A soldier of proved valor, he was entrusted with the defense of the city.

X Young and energetic, the task seemed easy to me.

☺ Young and energetic, I thought the task easy.

X Without a friend to counsel him, the temptation proved irresistible.

☺ Without a friend to counsel him, he found the temptation irresistible.

Sentences violating this rule are often confusing and difficult for the reader to understand.

X Being in a dilapidated condition, I was able to buy the house very cheap.

X Wondering irresolutely what to do next, the clock struck twelve.

Chapter 2

ELEMENTARY PRINCIPLES OF COMPOSITION

Rule 8. Make the paragraph the unit of composition.

Write one paragraph to each topic. A paragraph expresses a complete thought.

If the subject on which you are writing is of a trivial nature, or if you intend to treat it very briefly, there may be no need to subdivide it into topics. Thus. a brief description, a brief book review, a brief account of a single incident, the expressing of a single idea, any one of these is best written in a single paragraph. After the paragraph has been written, examine it to see whether you can improve the clarity by subdividing it.

In most other cases, a subject should be subdivided into topics, and each topic should be made the subject of a paragraph. The point of doing this is, of course, to aid the reader. The beginning of each paragraph is a signal to the reader that a new step in the development of the subject has been reached.

The extent of subdivision required will vary with the length of the composition. For example, a short notice of a book or poem might consist of a single paragraph. One slightly longer might consist of two paragraphs:

First paragraph: account of the work

Second paragraph: critical discussion

A report on a poem, written for a literature class, might consist of seven paragraphs:

1. Facts of composition and publication

2. Kind of poem; metrical form

3. Subject

4. Treatment of subject

5. For what chiefly remarkable

6. Wherein characteristic of the writer

7. Relationship to other works

The contents of paragraphs 3 and 4 would vary with the poem. Usually, paragraph 3 would indicate the actual or imagined circumstances of the poem (the situation), if these call for explanation, and would then state the subject and outline its development. If the poem is a narrative in the third person throughout, paragraph 3 need contain no more than a concise summary of the action. Paragraph 4 would indicate the leading ideas and show how they are made prominent or would indicate what points in the narrative are mainly emphasized.

A novel might be discussed under the heads:

1. Setting

2. Plot

3. Characters

4. Purpose

An historical event might be discussed under the heads:

1. What led up to the event

2. Account of the event

3. What the event led up to

In treating either of these last two subjects, you would probably find it necessary to subdivide one or more of the suggested topics.

Generally speaking, single sentences should not be written or printed as paragraphs. One exception may be made in sentences of transition, indicating the relation between the parts of an exposition or argument. Frequent exceptions are also necessary in textbooks, guidebooks, and other works in which many topics are treated briefly.

In dialogue, each speech, even if only a single word, is a paragraph by itself. In other words, a new paragraph begins with each change of speaker. The application of this rule, when dialogue and narrative are combined, is best learned by studying examples in well-written works of fiction.

Rule 9. Begin each paragraph with a topic sentence.

Begin each paragraph with a topic sentence and end it in conformity with the beginning, although certain exceptions apply. Again, the object is to help the reader gain clarity and understanding of what you are writing. The practice recommended here enables readers to discover the purpose of each paragraph as they begin to read it, and to retain this purpose in mind as they end it. For this reason, the most useful kind of paragraph, particularly in exposition and argument, is that in which:

(a) the topic sentence comes at or near the beginning;

(b) the succeeding sentences explain, establish, or develop the statement made in the topic sentence; and

(c) the final sentence either emphasizes the thought of the topic sentence or states some important consequence.

Avoid ending with a digression or an unimportant detail.

If the paragraph forms part of a larger composition, its relation to what precedes, or its function as a part of the whole, may need to be expressed. This can be done sometimes by a mere word or phrase (*again*; *therefore*; *for the same reason*) in the topic sentence. Other times, however, it is expedient to precede the topic sentence by one or more sentences of introduction or transition. If more than one such sentence is required, it is generally better to set apart the transitional sentences as a separate paragraph.

According to the message you are trying to communicate in your writing, you may, as indicated above, relate the body of the paragraph to the topic sentence in one or more of several different ways. You may make the meaning of the topic sentence clearer by restating it in other forms; by defining its terms; by denying the contrary; or by giving illustrations or specific instances. Similarly, you may establish it by proofs; or you may develop it by showing its implications and consequences. In a long paragraph, you may carry out several of these processes.

Consider the following:

> [1] Now, to be properly enjoyed, a walking tour should be gone upon alone. [2] If you go in a company, or even in pairs, it is no longer a walking tour in anything but name; it is something else and more in the nature of a picnic. [3] A walking tour should be gone upon alone, because freedom is of the essence; because you should be able to stop and go on, and follow this way or that, as the freak takes you; and because you must have your own pace, and neither trot alongside a champion walker, nor mince in time with a girl. [4] And you must be open to all impressions and let your thoughts take color from what you see. [5] You should be as a pipe for any wind to play upon. [6] "I cannot see the wit," says Hazlitt, "of walking and talking at the same time. [7] When I am in the country, I wish to vegetate like the country," which is the gist of all that can be said upon the matter. [8] There should be no cackle of voices at your elbow, to jar on the meditative silence of the morning. [9] And so long as a

man is reasoning he cannot surrender himself to that fine intoxication that comes of much motion in the open air, that begins in a sort of dazzle and sluggishness of the brain, and ends in a peace that passes comprehension. — Stevenson, *Walking Tours*.

Let's break down the sentences comprising this paragraph.

1. Topic sentence.

2. The meaning made clearer by denial of the contrary.

3. The topic sentence repeated, in abridged form, and supported by three reasons; the meaning of the third ("you must have your own pace") made clearer by denying the contrary.

4. A fourth reason, stated in two forms.

5. The same reason, stated in still another form.

6–7. The same reason as stated by Hazlitt.

8. Repetition, in paraphrase, of the quotation from Hazlitt.

9. Final statement of the fourth reason, in language amplified and heightened to form a strong conclusion.

Let's consider another example:

[1] It was chiefly in the eighteenth century that a very different conception of history grew up. [2] Historians then came to believe that their task was not so much to paint a picture as to solve a problem; to explain or illustrate the successive phases of national growth, prosperity, and adversity. [3] The history of morals, of industry, of intellect, and of art; the changes that take place in manners or beliefs; the dominant ideas that prevailed in successive periods; the rise, fall, and modification of political constitutions; in a word, all

the conditions of national well-being became the subject of their works. [4] They sought rather to write a history of peoples than a history of kings. [5] They looked especially in history for the chain of causes and effects. [6] They undertook to study in the past the physiology of nations, and hoped by applying the experimental method on a large scale to deduce some lessons of real value about the conditions on which the welfare of society mainly depend.

—Lecky, *The Political Value of History*

Again, breaking down the paragraph, we have:

1. Topic sentence.

2. The meaning of the topic sentence made clearer; the new conception of history defined.

3. The definition expanded.

4. The definition explained by contrast.

5. The definition supplemented: another element in the new conception of history.

6. Conclusion: an important consequence of the new conception of history.

In narration and description, the paragraph sometimes begins with a concise, comprehensive statement serving to hold together the details that follow.

The breeze served us admirably.

The campaign opened with a series of reverses.

The next ten or twelve pages were filled with a curious set of entries.

But this device, if too often used, can become a mannerism. More commonly the opening sentence simply indicates by its subject with what the paragraph is to be principally concerned.

> At length I thought I might return towards the stockade.

> He picked up the heavy lamp from the table and began to explore.

> Another flight of steps, and they emerged on the roof.

The brief paragraphs of animated narrative, however, are often without even this semblance of a topic sentence. The break between them serves the purpose of a rhetorical pause, making prominent some detail of the action.

Rule 10. Use the active voice.

The active voice is usually more direct and vigorous than the passive:

> ☺ I shall always remember my visit to Boston.

This is much better than:

> ✗ My visit to Boston will always be remembered by me.

The latter sentence is less direct, less bold, and less concise. If the writer tries to make it more concise by omitting *by me*,

> ✗ My first visit to Boston will always be remembered.

it becomes indefinite: is it the writer, or some undisclosed person, or the world at large, who will always remember this visit?

This rule does not mean that the writer should entirely discard the passive voice, which is often convenient and sometimes necessary.

> ☺ The dramatists of the Restoration are little esteemed today.

☺ Modern readers have little esteem for the dramatists of the Restoration.

The first would be the right form in a paragraph on the dramatists of the Restoration; the second, in a paragraph on the tastes of modern readers. The need to make a particular word the subject of a sentence will often, as in these examples, determine which voice is appropriate to use.

As a rule, avoid making one passive depend directly upon another.

✕ Gold was not allowed to be exported.

☺ It was forbidden to export gold (The export of gold was prohibited).

✕ He has been proved to have been seen entering the building.

☺ It has been proved that he was seen to enter the building.

In both of these examples, before correction, the word properly related to the second passive is made the subject of the first.

A common fault is to use as the subject of a passive construction a noun that expresses the entire action, leaving to the verb no function other than completing the sentence.

✕ A survey of this region was made in 1900.

☺ This region was surveyed in 1900.

✕ Mobilization of the army was rapidly effected.

☺ The army was rapidly mobilized.

✕ Confirmation of the facts cannot be obtained.

☺ These facts cannot be confirmed.

Compare the sentence in the first set of examples, "The export of gold was prohibited," in which the predicate "was prohibited" expresses something not implied in "export."

The habitual use of active voice makes for forcible writing. This is true not only in narrative mainly concerned with action, but in writing of any kind. Many bland descriptive sentences can be made lively and more emphatic by substituting a verb in the active voice for some such perfunctory expression as *there is* or *could be heard.*

✗ There were a great number of dead leaves lying on the ground.

☺ Dead leaves covered the ground.

✗ The sound of a guitar somewhere in the house could be heard.

☺ Somewhere in the house a guitar hummed.

✗ The reason that he left college was that his health became impaired.

☺ Failing health compelled him to leave college.

✗ It was not long before he was very sorry that he had said what he had.

☺ He soon regretted his words.

Rule 11. Put statements in positive form.

Make definite assertions in your writing. Avoid bland, colorless, hesitating, non-committal language. Use the word *not* as a means of denial or in antithesis, never as a means of evasion.

✗ He was not very often on time.

☺ He usually came late.

✗ He did not think studying Latin was much use.

☺ He thought the study of Latin useless.

✗ *The Taming of the Shrew* is rather weak in spots. Shakespeare does not portray Katharine as a very admirable character, nor does Bianca remain long in memory as an important character in Shakespeare's works.

☺ The women in *The Taming of the Shrew* are unattractive. Katharine is disagreeable, Bianca insignificant.

The last example, before correction, is indefinite as well as negative. The corrected version, consequently, is merely a guess at the writer's intention.

All three examples show the weakness inherent in the word *not*. Consciously or unconsciously, the reader is dissatisfied with being told only what is not; he wishes to be told what is. Therefore, as a rule, it is better to express even a negative in positive form.

✗ **Weak**	☺ **Strong**
not honest	dishonest
not important	trifling
Did not remember	Forgot
Did not pay attention to	ignored

The antithesis of negative and positive is strong, and in writing, we can express the essence of this in:

☺ Not charity, but simple justice.

☺ Not that I loved Caesar less, but Rome more.

Negative words other than *not* are usually strong:

☺ The sun never sets upon the British flag.

Rule 12. Use definite, specific, concrete language.

Prefer the specific to the general, the definite to the vague, the concrete to the abstract.

✕ A period of unfavorable weather set in.

☺ It rained every day for a week.

✕ He showed satisfaction as he took possession of his well-earned reward.

☺ He grinned as he pocketed the coin.

✕ There is a general agreement among those who have enjoyed the experience that surf-riding is productive of great exhilaration.

☺ All who have tried surf-riding agree that it is most exhilarating.

If those who have studied the art of writing are in accord on any one point, it is on this: The surest method of arousing and holding the reader's attention is by being specific, definite, and concrete. Critics have pointed out how much of the effectiveness of great writers such as Homer, Dante, and Shakespeare results from their definiteness and concreteness. Browning, another great author, gives the reader many striking examples. Take, for instance, the lines from *My Last Duchess:*

Sir, 'twas all one! My favor at her breast,

The dropping of the daylight in the west,

The bough of cherries some officious fool

Broke in the orchard for her, the white mule

She rode with round the terrace—all and each

Would draw from her alike the approving speech,

Or blush, at least,

and those that end the poem,

Notice Neptune, though,

Taming a sea-horse, thought a rarity,

Which Claus of Innsbruck cast in bronze for me.

These words evoke vivid mental pictures. Recall how in *The Bishop Orders his Tomb in St. Praxed's Church*, "the Renaissance spirit—its worldliness, inconsistency, pride, hypocrisy, ignorance of itself, love of art, of luxury, of good Latin," to quote Ruskin's comment on the poem, is made manifest in specific details and in concrete terms.

Prose, in particular narrative and descriptive prose, is made vivid by the same means. If the experiences of Jim Hawkins and of David Balfour, of Kim, of Nostromo, have seemed for the moment real to countless readers, if in reading Carlyle we have almost the sense of being physically present at the taking of the Bastille, it is because of the definiteness of the details and the concreteness of the terms used. It is not that every detail is given—that would be impossible and would serve no purpose—but that all the significant details are given, and not vaguely, but with such definiteness that the reader, in imagination, can project himself into the scene.

In exposition and in argument, you must likewise never lose your hold upon the concrete. Even when you are dealing with general principles, you must give instances of their application.

"This superiority of specific expressions is clearly due to the effort required to translate words into thoughts. As we do not think in generals, but in particulars—as whenever any class of things is referred to, we represent it to ourselves by calling to mind individual members of it, it follows that when an abstract word is used, the listener or reader has to choose, from his stock of images, one or more by which he may figure to himself the genus mentioned. In doing this, some delay must arise, some force be expended; and if by employing a specific term an appropriate image can be at once suggested, an economy is achieved, and a more vivid impression produced."

Herbert Spencer, from whose *Philosophy of Style* the above passage is quoted, illustrates the principle by the sentences:

> "In proportion as the manners, customs, and amusements of a nation are cruel and barbarous, the regulations of their penal code will be severe."

> "In proportion as men delight in battles, bullfights, and combats of gladiators, will they punish by hanging, burning, and the rack."

Rule 13. Omit needless words.

Vigorous writing is concise. A sentence should contain no unnecessary words, a paragraph no unnecessary sentences, for the same reason that a drawing should have no unnecessary lines and a machine no unnecessary parts. This requires not that the writer make all his sentences short, or that he avoid all detail and treat his subjects only in outline, but that he make every word tell.

Many expressions in common use violate this principle:

✕ Word clutter	☺ Concise form
the question as to whether	Whether
there is no doubt but that	no doubt (doubtless)
used for fuel purposes	used for fuel
he is a man who	he
in a hasty manner	hastily
this is a subject which	this subject
His story is a strange one.	His story is strange.

In particular, the expression *the fact that* should be deleted from every sentence in which it occurs.

✕ **Word clutter**	☺ **Concise form**
owing to the fact that	since (because)
in spite of the fact that	though (although)
call your attention to the fact that	remind you (notify you)
I was unaware of the fact that	I was unaware that (did not know)
the fact that he had failed	his failure

Who is, which was, and the like are often superfluous and should be written out of sentences.

> ✕ His brother, who is a member of the same firm
>
> ☺ His brother, a member of the same firm
>
> ✕ Trafalgar, which was Nelson's last battle
>
> ☺ Trafalgar, Nelson's last battle

Just as positive statement is more concise than negative, and active voice is more concise than the passive, many of the examples given under Rules 11 and 12 illustrate this principle as well.

A common violation of conciseness is the presentation of a single complex idea, step by step, in a series of sentences or independent clauses that might be more effectively combined into one.

> ✕ Macbeth was very ambitious. This led him to wish to become king of Scotland. The witches told him that this wish of his would come true. The king of Scotland at this time was Duncan. Encouraged by his wife, Macbeth murdered Duncan. He was thus enabled to succeed Duncan as king. (51 words.)

☺ Encouraged by his wife, Macbeth achieved his ambition and realized the prediction of the witches by murdering Duncan and becoming king of Scotland in his place. (26 words.)

✗ There were several less important courses, but these were the most important, and although they did not come every day, they came often enough to keep you in such a state of mind that you never knew what your next move would be. (43 words.)

☺ These, the most important courses of all, came, if not daily, at least often enough to keep one under constant strain. (21 words.)

Rule 14. Avoid a succession of loose sentences.

This rule refers especially to loose sentences of a particular type—those consisting of two coordinate clauses, the second introduced by a conjunction or relative. Although single sentences of this type may be acceptable (see Rule 4), a series soon becomes monotonous. An unskilled writer will sometimes construct a whole paragraph of such sentences, using as connectives *and, but, so,* and less frequently *who, which, when, where,* and *while,* these last in non-restrictive senses (see Rule 3).

The third concert of the subscription series was given last evening, and a large audience was in attendance. Mr. Edward Appleton was the soloist, and the Boston Symphony Orchestra furnished the instrumental music. The former showed himself to be an artist of the first rank, while the latter proved itself fully deserving of its high reputation. The interest aroused by the series has been very gratifying to the Committee, and it is planned to give a similar series annually hereafter. The fourth concert will be given on Tuesday, May 10, when an equally entertaining program will be presented.

Apart from the trite and empty nature of the above paragraph, it is weak because of the structure of its sentences, with their mechanical symmetry and sing-song. Contrast with them the sentences in the paragraphs quoted under Rule 9, or in any piece of good English prose, as the preface (Before the Curtain) to *Vanity Fair*.

If you find that you have written a series of sentences of the type described, you should recast enough of them to remove the monotony. Replace them with simple sentences, sentences of two clauses joined by a semicolon, by periodic sentences of two clauses, by sentences, loose or periodic, of three clauses— whichever best represent the real relations of the thought.

Rule 15. Express coordinate ideas in similar form.

This principle, that of parallel construction, requires that expressions of similar content and function should be outwardly similar. The likeness of form enables the reader to recognize more readily the likeness of content and function. The novice writer often violates this principle from a mistaken belief that he should constantly vary the form of his expressions. It is true that in repeating a statement in order to emphasize it, it may be desirable to vary its form. For illustration, see the paragraph from Stevenson quoted under Rule 9. But apart from this, the writer should follow the principle of parallel construction.

X Formerly, science was taught by the textbook method, while now the laboratory method is employed.

☺ Formerly, science was taught by the textbook method; now it is taught by the laboratory method.

The first version gives the impression that the writer is undecided or timid; he seems unable or afraid to choose one form of expression and hold to it. The second version shows that the writer has at least decided on the point he wants to make, and he makes it.

By this principle, an article or a preposition that applies to all the members of a series must either be used only before the first term or else be repeated before each term. In the following sentences, the first of the pair is missing an article, and the second of each is correctly written.

✗ The French, the Italians, Spanish, and Portuguese

☺ The French, the Italians, the Spanish, and the Portuguese

✗ In spring, summer, or in winter

☺ In spring, summer, or winter

☺ In spring, in summer, or in winter

Correlative expressions (*both, and*; *not, but*; *not only, but also*; *either, or*; *first, second, third*; and the like) should be followed by the same grammatical construction, that is, virtually, by the same part of speech. (Such combinations as "both Henry and I," "not silk, but a cheap substitute," are obviously within the rule.) Many violations of this rule (as the three below) arise from faulty arrangement; others (as the fourth example) from the use of unlike constructions.

✗ It was both a long ceremony and very tedious.

☺ The ceremony was both long and tedious.

✗ A time not for words, but action.

☺ A time not for words, but for action.

✗ My objections are, first, the injustice of the measure; second, that it is unconstitutional.

☺ My objections are, first, that the measure is unjust; second, that it is unconstitutional.

✗ Either you must grant his request or incur his wrath.

☺ You must either grant his request or incur his wrath.

See also the third example under Rule 12 and the last under Rule 13.

What if you need to express a very large number of similar ideas, say twenty? Must you write twenty consecutive sentences of the same pattern? On closer examination, you will probably find that the difficulty is imaginary, that your twenty ideas can be classified in groups, and that you need apply the principle only within each group. Otherwise, it is best to avoid difficulty by putting your statements in the form of a table.

Rule 16. Keep related words together.

The position of words in a sentence is the principal means of showing their relationship. You must therefore try to bring together the words, and groups of words, that are related in thought, and keep apart those which are not so related.

The subject of a sentence and the principal verb should not, as a rule, be separated by a phrase or clause that can be written at the beginning.

✗ Wordsworth, in the fifth book of *The Excursion*, gives a minute description of this church.

☺ In the fifth book of *The Excursion*, Wordsworth gives a minute description of this church.

✗ Cast iron, when treated in a Bessemer converter, is changed into steel.

☺ By treatment in a Bessemer converter, cast iron is changed into steel.

The objection is that the interposed phrase or clause needlessly interrupts the natural order of the main clause. Usually, however, this objection does not hold when the order is interrupted only by a relative clause or by an expression in apposition. Nor does it hold in periodic sentences in which the interruption is a deliberately used means of creating suspense (see examples under Rule 18).

Usually, the relative pronoun should come immediately after its antecedent. Note, too, that in almost every instance, starting a sentence with "There is" or any similar form of the expression should be avoided.

✗ There was a look in his eye that boded mischief.

☺ In his eye was a look that boded mischief.

✗ He wrote three articles about his adventures in Spain, which were published in *Harper's Magazine*.

☺ He published in *Harper's Magazine* three articles about his adventures in Spain.

✗ This is a portrait of Benjamin Harrison, grandson of William Henry Harrison, who became President in 1889.

☺ This is a portrait of Benjamin Harrison, grandson of William Henry Harrison. He became President in 1889.

A noun in apposition may come between antecedent and relative, because in such a combination no real ambiguity can arise.

The Duke of York, his brother, who was regarded with hostility by the Whigs

Modifiers should come, if possible, next to the word they modify. If several expressions modify the same word, they should be so arranged to avoid ambiguity or confusing the reader.

✗ All the members were not present.

☺ Not all the members were present.

✗ He only found two mistakes.

☺ He found only two mistakes.

✗ Major R. E. Joyce will give a lecture on Tuesday evening in Bailey Hall, to which the public is invited, on "My Experiences in Mesopotamia" at 8 p.m.

☺ On Tuesday at 8 p.m., Major R. E. Joyce will give in Bailey Hall a lecture on "My Experiences in Mesopotamia." The public is invited.

Rule 17. In summaries, keep to one tense.

In summarizing the action of a drama, you should always use the present tense. In summarizing a poem, story, or novel, you should preferably use the present, though you may use the past if you prefer. If the summary is in the present tense, antecedent action should be expressed by the perfect; if in the past, by the past perfect.

> An unforeseen chance prevents Friar John from delivering Friar Lawrence's letter to Romeo. Meanwhile, owing to her father's arbitrary change of the day set for her wedding, Juliet has been compelled to drink the potion on Tuesday night, with the result that Balthasar informs Romeo of her supposed death before Friar Lawrence learns of the non-delivery of the letter.

But whichever tense is used in the summary, a past tense in indirect discourse or in indirect question should remain unchanged.

> The Friar confesses that it was he who married them.

Apart from the exceptions noted, whichever tense you choose, you should use throughout. Shifting from one tense to the other gives the appearance of uncertainty and lack of clarity (compare Rule 15).

In presenting the statements or the thought of someone else, as in summarizing an essay or reporting a speech, you should avoid intercalating such expressions as "he said," "he stated," "the speaker added," "the speaker then went on to say," and the like. Indicate clearly right from the start that what follows is summary, and then waste no words in repeating the notification.

In newspapers and in many kinds of textbooks, summaries of one kind or another may be indispensable, and it is a useful exercise for children in primary schools to retell a story in their own words. But in the criticism or interpretation of literature, you should be careful to avoid dropping into summary. You may find it necessary to devote one or two sentences to indicating the subject, or the opening situation, of the work you are discussing; you may cite numerous details to illustrate its qualities. But you should aim to write an orderly discussion supported by evidence, not a summary with occasional comment. Similarly, if the scope of your discussion includes a number of works, you will as a rule do better not to take them up singly in chronological order but to aim from the beginning at establishing general conclusions.

Rule 18. Place the emphatic words of a sentence at the end.

The proper place in a sentence for the word, or group of words, that you want to make most prominent is usually the end.

> ✗ Humanity has hardly advanced in fortitude since that time, though it has advanced in many other ways.

> ☺ Humanity, since that time, has advanced in many other ways, but it has hardly advanced in fortitude.

X This steel is principally used for making razors, because of its hardness.

☺ Because of its hardness, this steel is principally used in making razors.

The word or group of words entitled to this position of prominence is usually the logical predicate, that is, the *new* element in the sentence, as in the second example.

The effectiveness of the periodic sentence arises from the prominence which it gives to the main statement.

> Four centuries ago, Christopher Columbus, one of the Italian mariners whom the decline of their own republics had put at the service of the world and of adventure, seeking for Spain a westward passage to the Indies as a set-off against the achievements of Portuguese discoverers, lighted on America.

> With these hopes and in this belief I would urge you, laying aside all hindrance, thrusting away all private aims, to devote yourself unswervingly and unflinchingly to the successful prosecution of this war.

The other prominent position in the sentence is the beginning. Any element in the sentence, other than the subject, may become emphatic when placed first.

> Deceit or treachery he could never forgive.

> So vast and rude, fretted by the action of nearly three thousand years, the fragments of this architecture may often seem, at first sight, like works of nature.

A subject written first in its sentence may be emphatic, but hardly by its position alone. In this sentence,

> Great kings worshipped at his shrine,

the emphasis upon *kings* arises largely from its meaning and from the context. To receive special emphasis, the subject of a sentence must take the position of the predicate.

> Through the middle of the valley flowed a winding stream.

The principle that the proper place for what is to be made most prominent is the end applies equally to the words of a sentence, to the sentences of a paragraph, and to the paragraphs of a composition.

Chapter 3

BASIC RULES OF CAPITALIZATION

C apital letters emphasize certain words to distinguish them from the surrounding text. The rules for capitalization in English grammar are reasonably straightforward. However, some writers overboard with capitalizing words that should be written in lowercase; or they overlook proper nouns that should be capitalized. Either way, such errors give the appearance of an unpolished manuscript. The basic rules of capitalization given in this chapter will help you to produce a clean and grammatically correct final draft.

➡ *Editor's Note:* This chapter did not appear in the first edition of Strunk's *Elements of Style,* but it has been included in this edition because capitalization rules are a source of confusion for many writers. This chapter is excerpted from *Elements of Style 2017* https://amazon.com/dp/B01MD0396I

Rule 19. "First Word" Capitalization Rules.

Capitalize the first word of every complete sentence.

Life is what you make it.

The Internet has revolutionized the world.

I think...therefore I am.

Capitalize the first word of a sentence fragment and any single word that stands alone in running copy.

What the heck...

Umm...

Capitalize the first word of every quotation.

Mark demanded, "Stop the car! Now!"

"Why do you want to know?" Naomi asked.

"I apologized," Lucy said, "but you did not accept it."

Capitalize the first word in every direct question.

Let me ask you; "How old are you?"

Who are you? Are you the detective Donald hired?

"Where are my car keys?" Carole asked.

Capitalize a one-word interjection or interrogatory when it stands alone in running text.

Oh! I forgot to call you.

Really?

Argh! Facebook blocked my account.

If the first word of a sentence is a trademark, an acronym, or a proper noun usually written in lower case, capitalize it. Notice how the trademarked names *iPhone* and *eBay* are handled in these examples:

IPhone users may buy iPhone apps from the iStore.

EBay is a popular site. Julio bought his iPad on eBay.

Capitalize the first word of every numbered clause, regardless of how the clauses are structured in the paragraph. Consider the two examples below, where the first presents the clauses as a series of paragraphs, and the second illustrates numbered clauses in running text:

The defendant claims that:

(1) He did not attack the man;

(2) The witness appeared drunk at the time;

(3) In fact, the witness himself attacked the man.

The witness asserts under oath that: (1) He saw the man attacked; (2) He saw him fall; (3) He saw the defendant flee.

Capitalize the first word in every line of a poem.

If you can keep your head when all about you
Are losing theirs and blaming it on you,
If you can trust yourself when all men doubt you,
But make allowance for their doubting too;
If you can wait and not be tired by waiting,
Or being lied about, don't deal in lies,
Or being hated, don't give way to hating,
And yet don't look too good, nor talk too wise...

—excerpt from Rudyard Kipling's *If*

Rule 20. Capitalize Proper Nouns.

Capitalize the names of people, places, holidays, and other proper nouns.

David Smith	Caesar	Easter
Queen Mary	Mount Shasta	Pacific Ocean

Capitalize the names of cities, states, provinces, and countries, but do not capitalize common nouns that refer to them, such as "city" in the phrase "city of Denver."

I live in the city of Denver.

He moved to the state of California.

Vancouver is in the province of British Columbia.

Ontario is one of the Canadian provinces.

Capitalize words derived from proper names.

American	Canadian	Martian
Irish whiskey	Jesuit priest	Greek statue

Capitalize the names of political parties, religious denominations, and schools of thought.

Democrat	Republican	Quaker
Catholic	Presbyterian	Methodist
Buddhist	Freemason	Wiccan

Capitalize assumed names and names given for distinction.

Attila the Hun	John Doe
Vlad the Impaler	John the Baptist
Alexander the Great	Spartacus

Capitalize a title when it precedes a person's name. When the title follows the person's name, it is a common noun and it should be written in lower case.

Donald Trump, president of the U.S., toured the city.

The mayor gave President Trump a tour of the city.

The president of the United States vetoed the bill.

Chairman Mark Murphy adjourned the meeting.

The chairman of Murphy Oil Corp. will retire next year.

Always capitalize the pronoun *I* and its various contractions, such as *I'm, I'll*, and *I've*.

I have two cats and no dogs.

I'd love to go on vacation!

I've lost my car keys.

I'll learn grammar eventually!

Rule 21. Capitalize Days, Months, and Historic Eras.

Capitalize the days of the week, months of the year, and both the day and month when they appear together in a date.

Monday, Tuesday, Wednesday, etc.

January, February, March, etc.

She was born on Thursday, February 1, 1962.

Capitalize words that refer to significant events or periods in human history.

Industrial Revolution	Civil War
Middle Ages	Stone Age
The Great Flood	Magna Carta
Vietnam War	Ice Age

Rule 22. When to Capitalize Landmarks.

Do not capitalize words such as river, mountain, sea, etc., when they are used as common nouns. But when used with an adjective or adjunct to specify a particular location, they become proper names and should be capitalized.

Mississippi River	the overflowing river
Mediterranean Sea	the towering mountains
Alleghany Mountains	the ocean waves

Rule 23. When to Capitalize the Names of Seasons.

Capitalize the names of the four seasons when they are used as proper nouns, in a title or headline, and when used as a "personified" noun (see Rule 24). Otherwise, do not capitalize the names of the four seasons. These usages are correct:

The summer was hot, the fall breezy, the winter frigid.

The Winter of my discontent

Will you be taking summer classes?

Cindy enjoys baking pies and cakes in the winter.

The Monterey Summer Festival

➡ A specific event, and a proper noun, so capitalize.

I plan to attend three summer music festivals.

➡ These festivals are generic, so use lowercase.

Rule 24. Capitalize "Personified" Nouns.

"Personification" is a concept in which inanimate objects are represented as having life and action. A personified noun is a proper noun and should be capitalized.

Clear-eyed Day broke on the horizon.

The Redwood said to the Oak, "I am taller than you."

The starry Night shook the dew from her wings.

Then Winter—with her virgin snow—settled over the town.

Rule 25. Capitalize Cardinal Points (Sometimes).

The cardinal points (north, south, east, and west) are common nouns and not capitalized. But when used to distinguish a specific location or region, they are proper nouns and should be capitalized.

The North fought against the South.

I will be traveling in the West.

The Middle East

If you go west in California, you will reach the ocean.

Rule 26. Capitalize Most Words in Titles.

Capitalize the first word and the last word of the title of a book, film, song, or other creative work. Capitalize all nouns, pronouns, adjectives, verbs, adverbs, and subordinating conjunctions. Capitalize prepositions only if they are used adverbially or adjectivally; otherwise, write prepositions lower case. Likewise, lower case articles (*a, an, the*), coordinating conjunctions, and the word *to* in an infinitive, such as "How to Play the Violin."

> *The Lord of the Rings*
>
> Apocalypse Orphan
>
> *The Creation of Adam*

Rule 27. When to Capitalize Roman Numerals.

Capitalize Roman numerals when they are part of a proper name, a title, or a chapter heading.

World War II	Pope John Paul II
Elizabeth II	Section III
Chapter V	Plate X

Rule 28. Capitalize Trademarks and Service Marks.

Trademarks and service marks are proper nouns and should be capitalized. Product names officially spelled with a first letter that is lowercased, such as iPhone, are exceptions to this rule and should follow that convention (but see Rule 19 for another exception). Include the legal symbol after the mark with no space between them. These symbols are acceptable: ™, (tm), (TM), and SM, (sm), (SM). Note that ™ and SM are preferred, but all the examples below are correct.

Kleenex™	Band-Aid(tm)
Clorox(TM)	WalmartSM
Citicorp(sm)	Yahoo!(SM)

Rule 29. When to Capitalize Relative Words.

When relative (or family) words such as *mother, father, brother, sister,* and *uncle* are used as common nouns, do not capitalize these words; but read on for several exceptions.

> Julia's father would not let her go to the party.
>
> My mother was arrested; now she is in jail.

I could not remember my aunt's last name!

When a relative word is used with a person's name, and no possessive pronoun is used, capitalize the word.

I called Uncle Joe to ask for a loan, but he refused.

I have not seen Aunt Crystal for years.

My mother says Grandpa Julio is filthy rich.

When a relative word is preceded by a possessive pronoun (*my, her, his, your, their*), it is a common noun, so write it in lowercase, even if it is used with a person's name. This rule conforms to Chicago Style; other style guides may offer different advice.

I called my uncle Joe to ask for a loan, but he refused.

I have not seen her aunt Crystal for years.

My father Jake is a carpenter by profession.

Capitalize relative words when those words are substituted in place of a person's name.

You might not agree, but Father knows best.

Her father Jake works hard to earn a living.

Did you buy a present for your mother?

Yes, I bought these videos for Mother.

➡ **TIP:** If you replace the relative word in a sentence with the person's name and the sentence still reads correctly, the relative word is a proper noun and should be capitalized. Consider this example:

Did you buy a present for *Mother*?

Did you buy a present for *Ruth*?

The relative word m*other* can be replaced with *Ruth* and this sentence still reads correctly; therefore, *mother* is a proper noun and should be capitalized. But in the two examples below, switching *mother* and *Ruth* doesn't work, so *mother* is a common noun and not capitalized.

Did you buy a present for your *mother*?

Did you buy a present for your *Ruth*?

Rule 30. Capitalize Some Religious Titles and Terms.

Pronouns that refer to the Supreme Being should be written in lowercase, according to Chicago Style. But the Chicago Style website notes that some religious writers and readers may be offended by this practice. The best approach is to follow "house rules" of the publisher, or consider the audience and write pronouns that refer to the Supreme Being in uppercase or lowercase as appropriate for that particular audience.

The miracle of life is His work.

I trust that He will guide me.

Capitalize the names that refer to Christ.

Jesus Christ, Son of God, Man of Galilee, The Crucified, The Anointed One, Savior

Capitalize the names of God in all religions.

Christianity: God, Lord, Creator, Providence, Holy One, Almighty, Heavenly Father, God the Father

Judaism: Jehova, Yahweh, Adonai, YHWH, EL, Elohim, Eloah, El Shaddai, Tzevaot, Sabaoth

Islam: Allah; the 99 Names of God—Ar Rahman (The All Merciful); Al Malik (The King, The Sovereign); and others.

Hinduism: Brahma, Vishnu, Shiva, Rama, Krishna, Ganapati, Lakshmi, Indra, Surya, Agni, and others.

Do not capitalize nonspecific uses of the word *god.*

Zeus was the god of the sky and thunder in Greece.

The king of the gods, Zeus, ruled from Mount Olympus.

In Katmandu, Nepal, a group of young girls are worshipped as goddesses.

Capitalize the names of deities and religious figures.

Virgin Mary	Greek gods	Shiva
Moses	Muhammad	Buddha
Zeus	Poseidon	gods of Rome

Capitalize the various names of God's evil detractor.

Beelzebub, Prince of Darkness, Satan, King of Hell, Devil, Tempter of Men, Father of Lies, Dark Lord, Evil One

Capitalize the names and designations of characters in the Bible and in the scriptures of other religions.

Lily of Israel, Rose of Sharon, Comfortress of the Afflicted, Help of Christians, Prince of the Apostles, Star of the Sea, John the Baptist

Capitalize proper nouns that refer to the Bible or to the scriptures of other religions, and to any parts of those texts.

Christianity: Holy Writ, Sacred Book, Holy Book, God's Word, Old Testament, New Testament, Gospel of St. Matthew.

Judaism: Hebrew Bible, Tanakh, Torah, Nevi'im

Hinduism: Shruti, Vedas, Riveda, Aranyakas, Brahmanas, Upanishads, Bhagavad Gita,

Buddhism: Dhammapada, Tripitaka

Taoism: Tao Te Ching, Chuang Tzu, I Ching

Islam: The Qur'an, Hadith, Sunnah

Rule 31. When to Capitalize Political Titles.

Capitalize the titles of honorable, state, and political offices when used as part of a formal title. Otherwise, write these titles as common nouns and use lowercase.

President Donald Trump toured the factory.

Barack Obama was elected president in 2008.

The company's leader is Chairman Mark Murphy.

Mark Murphy is chairman of the company.

Capitalize political titles and other official titles that directly precede names, but do not capitalize titles and designations that follow names.

Carolyn worked as assistant to Mayor Thompson.

I interviewed Gerald Thompson, mayor of Boston.

Capitalize the names of military organizations, bases, etc.

U.S. Army	3rd Regiment
the Army	the Navy
U.S. Navy	French Army
British Navy	Marine Corps
the Marines	the Air Force
U.S. Air Force	Royal Air Force

Capitalize acronyms formed from the initials of countries, organizations, and well-known treaties.

FBI	CIA	USA
UN	NSA	EU
UNESCO	NATO	NAFTA

Capitalize most acronyms formed from the first letters of several words, such as FYI, FAQ, and ASAP when written in running text and dialogue. However, acronyms commonly used in Internet discussion, chat, and mobile texting are commonly written as either uppercase or lowercase.

Rule 32. When to Capitalize Educational Titles.

Do not capitalize the words freshman, sophomore, junior, or senior unless used at the beginning of a sentence or in a headline. When referring to students, upper-division is preferred to upper-class.

Capitalize the names of colleges and universities. But the terms "university" and "college" when used alone usually are common nouns and should not be capitalized. The usages below are correct:

> Harvard University
>
> College of the Canyons
>
> The university student flunked his grammar course because he failed the exam.
>
> Ask the college bookstore to stock this book.

Capitalize the names of college and university departments, and official bodies of educational organizations.

> The School of Law is also called the law school.
>
> The Board of Regents decided to raise the tuition.
>
> The School of Education grants teaching degrees to graduates.
>
> I attended the University of California at Northridge.
>
> When I attended the college, I took science courses.

Capitalize letter grades earned in courses.

That girl should receive an A for effort.

He earned an F in math because he failed the exam.

Betty has a C average in Spanish, she can do better.

Lowercase academic degrees when used generically.

She received a law degree from Harvard University.

Allan is pursuing a bachelor's degree at Yale.

You must have a master's degree to apply for this job.

He earned a doctorate from Stanford University.

Capitalize educational degrees only when they directly precede ˙ or follow a person's name; otherwise, use lowercase (Chicago Style); or capitalize all degree names no matter where they appear (AP Style).

Chicago Manual of Style:

Elizabeth earned a master of science degree from Harvard University.

Allan is pursuing a bachelor of education degree.

You need a bachelor in chemistry for this job.

but...

Bachelor of Education Allan Jones will speak today.

He introduced Lian Chen, Master of Journalism.

AP Style:

Elizabeth earned a Master of Science degree from Harvard University.

Allan is pursuing a Bachelor of Education degree.

You need a Bachelor in Chemistry for this job.

and...

Bachelor of Education Allan Jones will speak today.

He introduced Lian Chen, Master of Journalism.

Academic degree abbreviations require capitalization. The rules vary, depending on the style guide. For example:

Chicago Style	AP Style
PhD	Ph.D.
MA	M.A.
MS	M.S.
BS	B.S.
AA	A.A.

Rule 33. When to Capitalize Job Titles.

The rules for capitalizing job titles can be confusing. Generally, use lowercase for titles when preceded by an article (*a/an* or *the*); and all titles used as common nouns.

Mr. Carlson is the editorial director for the Los Angeles Times.

Mr. Carlson, Editorial Director of the Los Angeles Times, spoke at the luncheon.

Bill Gates is the chairman of Microsoft Corp.

Bill Gates, Chairman of Microsoft Corp., previewed the new Windows software.

Mr. Adams was the director of Z-Media Group, but he retired.

Mr. Adams, Director of Z-Media Group, has retired.

Do not capitalize generic occupational descriptions, regardless of whether they precede or follow the person's name.

When writer Steven Clark met with publisher Jules Martinique, they decided to launch a new imprint devoted to cook books, led by editor Joe Wilson.

When a person has an unusually long title, write the title after the name and in lowercase to avoid excessive capitalization that would look odd and be difficult to read.

X Special Assistant to the Director of Campus Projects Allan McDonald will be given new job duties when the fall semester begins.

➡ The job title in the example above contains numerous capital letters, making the sentence construction awkward.

☺ Allan McDonald, special assistant to the director of campus projects, will be given new job duties when the fall semester begins.

➡ Placing a long title after a person's name, set off by commas, and writing it in lowercase is easier on the eyes and flows better.

When a job title is part of an address or headline, capitalize the title, even if it is written after the name.

Craig Carson, Director of Public Affairs
Dept. of Building and Safety
P.O. Box 123456
Los Angeles CA 90010

Chapter 4

A FEW MATTERS OF FORM

Headings. Leave a blank line after the title or heading of a manuscript. On succeeding pages, begin typing on the first line.

Numerals. Do not spell out dates or serial numbers. Write them in figures or Roman notation, as may be appropriate.

✗ August Ninth, 1918

☺ August 9, 1918

✗ Nine August 1918

☺ 9 August 1918

✗ Rule Seven

☺ Rule 7

✗ Act Three

☺ Act III

✗ Three Hundred Fifty Second Infantry

☺ 352nd Infantry

Parentheses. A sentence containing an expression in parenthesis should be punctuated, outside of the marks of parenthesis, exactly as if the expression in parenthesis were absent. The expression within is punctuated as if it stood by itself, except that the final stop is omitted unless it is a question mark or an exclamation point.

I went to his house yesterday (my third attempt to see him), but he had left town.

He declares (and why should we doubt his good faith?) that he is now certain of success.

(When a wholly detached expression or sentence is parenthesized, such as this example, the final stop is written before the last mark of parenthesis.)

Hyphenation. If room exists at the end of a line for one or more syllables of a word but not for the whole word, divide the word, unless it involves cutting off only a single letter, or cutting off only two letters of a long word.

No hard and fast hyphenation rules for all words exist, but the most frequently cited principles are:

1. Divide the word according to its formation:

   know-ledge (not knowl-edge);
   Shake-speare (not Shakes-peare);
   atmo-sphere (not atmos-phere).

2. Divide on the vowel:

   edi-ble (not ed-ible); propo-sition; ordi-nary;
   reli-gious; oppo-nents; regu-lar; deco-rative;
   classi-fi-ca-tion (three divisions allowable);

3. Divide between double letters, unless they come at the end of the simple form of the word:

   Apen-nines; Cincin-nati; refer-ring; but tell-ing

4. Do not divide before final -*ed* if the *e* is silent::

   treat-ed (but not roam-ed or nam-ed)

The proper handling of consonants in combination is best illustrated by examples:

for-tune; pic-ture; sin-gle; presump-tuous;
illus-tration; sub-stan-tial (either division);
indus-try; instruc-tion; sug-ges-tion;

➡ *Editor's Note:* Just as grammar rules can change over time, so can hyphenation rules. Most writing guides today advise against breaking words of any length if fewer than three letters would remain on the current line or on the subsequent line. Thus, some of the above rules cited by Strunk, such as Rule 4 showing "treat-ed" as being correctly hyphenated, may not apply to your writing. Consult your preferred style guide for advice on hyphenation.

Quotations. Formal quotations cited as documentary evidence are introduced by a colon and enclosed in quotation marks.

> The provision of the Constitution is: "No tax or duty shall be laid on articles exported from any state."

Quotations of an entire line (or more) of verse, are begun on a fresh line and centered, but need not be enclosed in quotation marks.

> Wordsworth's enthusiasm for the Revolution was at first unbounded:
>
> Bliss was it in that dawn to be alive,
>
> But to be young was very heaven!

Quotations introduced by *that* are regarded as indirect discourse; do not enclose these passages in quotation marks.

✗ Keats declares that "Beauty is truth, truth beauty."

☺ Keats declares that beauty is truth, truth beauty.

Proverbial expressions and familiar phrases of literary origin require no quotation marks. The same is true of colloquialisms and slang.

These are the times that try men's souls.

He lives far from the madding crowd.

References. In scholarly work requiring exact references, abbreviate titles that occur frequently, giving the full forms in an alphabetical list at the end. As a general practice, give the references in parenthesis or in footnotes, not in the body of the sentence. Omit the words *act, scene, line, book, page, volume,* except when referring to only one of them, and punctuate as indicated below.

In the second scene of the third act

After the killing of Polonius, Hamlet is placed under guard (IV.ii. 14).

2 Samuel i:17–27

Othello II.iii. 264–267, III.iii. 155–161.

Chapter 5

WORDS AND EXPRESSIONS OFTEN MISUSED

S ome of the forms listed in this chapter, as *like I did*, are downright bad English; others, as *case, factor, feature, interesting, one of the most*, are good in their place, but are constantly obtruding themselves into places where their use is ill-advised. If you will make it your purpose from the beginning to express accurately your own individual thought, and you'll refuse to be satisfied with a ready-made formula that saves you the trouble of doing so, this last set of expressions will cause you little trouble. But if you find that in a careless moment you have used one of them, you should probably not patch up the sentence by substituting one word or set of words for another but recast it completely, as illustrated in a number of examples below.

All right. Idiomatic in familiar speech as a detached phrase in the sense, "Agreed," or "Go ahead." In other uses better avoided. Always written as two words. "Alright" is used in informal writing, but it is not a word and should not appear in an edited work.

As good or better than. Expressions of this type should be corrected by rearranging the sentence.

    ✗ My opinion is as good or better than his.

    ☺ My opinion is as good as his, or better.

    ☺ My opinion is as good as his, if not better.

As to whether. *Whether* is sufficient; see Rule 13.

Bid. Takes the infinitive without *to*. The past tense in the sense "ordered" is *bade*.

But. Unnecessary after *doubt* and *help*.

> ✗ I have no doubt but that
>
> ☺ I have no doubt that

> ✗ He could not help see but that
>
> ☺ He could not help seeing that

The overuse of *but* as a conjunction leads to the fault discussed earlier under Rule 14. A loose sentence formed with *but* can always be converted into a periodic sentence formed with *although*, as explained under Rule 4.

Particularly awkward is following one *but* by another, making a contrast to a contrast or a reservation to a reservation. This is easily corrected by re-arrangement.

> ✗ America had vast resources, but she seemed almost wholly unprepared for war. But within a year she had created an army of four million men.

> ☺ America seemed almost wholly unprepared for war, but she had vast resources. Within a year she had created an army of four million men.

Can. Means *am (is, are) able*. Do not use as a substitute for *may*.

Case. The *Concise Oxford Dictionary* begins its definition of this word: "instance of a thing's occurring; usual state of affairs." In these two senses, the word *case* and its plural form *cases* is usually unnecessary.

> ✗ In many cases, the rooms were left unclean.
>
> ☺ Many of the rooms were left unclean.

> ✗ It has rarely been the case that any mistake has been made.
>
> ☺ Few mistakes have been made.

Certainly. Used indiscriminately by some writers, much as others use *very*, to intensify any and every statement. A mannerism of this kind, bad in speech, is even worse in writing.

X It is certainly the truth,

☺ It is the truth.

X He certainly must eat to survive.

☺ He must eat to survive.

Character. Often simply redundant, used from a mere habit of wordiness.

X Acts of a hostile character

☺ Hostile acts

Claim, vb. With object-noun, means *lay claim to*. May be used with a dependent clause if this sense is clearly involved: *He claimed that he was the sole surviving heir.* (But even here, *claimed to be* would be better.) Not to be used as a substitute for *declare, maintain,* or *charge.*

Clever. This word has been greatly overused; it is best restricted to ingenuity displayed in small matters.

Compare. To *compare to* is to point out or imply resemblances between objects regarded as essentially of different order; to *compare with* is to point out differences between objects regarded as essentially of the same order. Thus, life has been compared to a pilgrimage, to a drama, to a battle; the U.S. Congress may be compared with the British Parliament. Paris has been compared to ancient Athens; it may be compared with modern London.

Consider. Not followed by *as* when it means "believe to be." "I consider him thoroughly competent." Compare, "The lecturer considered Cromwell first as soldier and second as administrator," where "considered" means "examined" or "discussed."

Data. A plural, like *phenomena* and *strata*.

☺ These data were tabulated.

➡ *Editor's Note:* This rule is obsolete. The word "data" today is commonly used as both a singular noun and a plural noun. So, it is acceptable to write using the singular form as well:

☺ This data is being reviewed.

Dependable. A needless substitute for *reliable, trustworthy.*

Different than. Not permissible. Substitute *different from, other than,* or *unlike.*

Divided into. Not to be misused for *composed of.* The line is sometimes difficult to draw: plays are divided into acts, but poems are composed of stanzas.

Don't. Contraction of *do not.* The contraction of *does not* is *doesn't.*

Due to. Incorrectly used for *through, because of,* or *owing to* in adverbial phrases:

✗ He lost the first game, due to carelessness.

In correct use related as predicate or as modifier to a particular noun:

☺ This invention is due to Edison.

Folk. A collective noun, equivalent to *people.* Use the singular form only.

Effect. As a noun, the word means *result*; as a verb, it means to *bring about, accomplish* (not to be confused with *affect,* which means "to influence").

Often loosely used as a noun in perfunctory writing about fashion, music, painting, and other arts: an Oriental effect; effects in pale green; very delicate effects; broad effects; subtle effects; a charming effect was produced by. The writer who has a definite meaning to express will not resort to such vague phrasing.

Etc. Equivalent to *and the rest, and so forth,* and not to be used if one of these would be insufficient, that is, if the reader would be left in doubt as to any important details. Least open to objection when it represents the last terms of a list already given in full, or immaterial words at the end of a quotation.

At the end of a list introduced by *such as, for example,* or any similar expression, *etc.* is incorrect.

Fact. Use this word only for matters capable of direct verification, not matters of judgment. That a certain event happened on a particular date, and that lead melts at a certain temperature, are facts. But such conclusions as that Napoleon was the greatest of modern generals, or that the climate of California is delightful, however incontestable they may be, are not properly facts.

Factor. A hackneyed word; the expressions of which it forms part can usually be replaced by something more direct and idiomatic.

X His superior training was the great factor in his winning the match.

☺ He won the match by being better trained.

X Heavy artillery has become an increasingly important factor in deciding battles.

☺ Heavy artillery has played a constantly larger part in deciding battles.

Feature. Another hackneyed word; like *factor,* it usually adds nothing to the sentence in which it occurs.

> ✗ A feature of the entertainment especially worthy of mention was the singing of Miss A.

> ☺ The entertainment included Miss A., whose singing was worthy of mention.

It is better to use the same number of words to tell what Miss A. sang, or if the program has been given, to tell how she sang.

As a verb, in the advertising sense of *offer as a special attraction*, it should be avoided.

Fix. Colloquial in American English for *arrange*, men, *prepare*. In technical and other formal writing, restrict it to its literary senses: *fasten, make firm or immovable*, etc.

Get. The colloquial *have got* for *have* should not be used in writing. The preferable form of the participle is *got*.

He is a man who. A common type of redundant expression; see Rule 13. This construction should be avoided.

> ✗ He is a man who is very ambitious.

> ☺ He is very ambitious.

> ✗ Spain is a country which I have always wanted to visit.

> ☺ I have always wanted to visit Spain.

However. In the meaning *nevertheless*, avoid using this word first in its sentence or clause.

> ✗ The roads were almost impassable. However, we at last succeeded in reaching camp.

> ☺ The roads were almost impassable. At last, however, we succeeded in reaching camp.

When *however* is written first, it means in whatever way or to whatever extent.

☺ However you advise him, he will probably do as he thinks best.

☺ However discouraging the prospect, he never lost heart.

Interesting. Avoid this word as a perfunctory means of introduction. Instead of announcing that what you are about to tell is interesting, make it so.

✗ An interesting story is told of

☺ (Tell the story without preamble.)

✗ In connection with the anticipated visit of Mr. B. to America

☺ Mr. B., who it is expected will soon visit America

Kind of. Not to be used as a substitute for *rather* (before adjectives and verbs), or except in familiar style, for *something like* (before nouns).

✗ Isaac is kind of angry today.

✗ I kind of thought I had passed my math test.

The two sentences above use *kind of* in place of *rather*, as, *Isaac is rather angry today*. The examples below are acceptable because *kind of* is used in the literal sense:

☺ I dislike that kind of notoriety.

☺ Amber is a kind of fossil resin.

The same rule applies to *sort of*.

Less. Should not be misused for *fewer*.

✗ He had less men than in the previous battle.

☺ He had fewer men than in the previous battle.

Less refers to quantity, *fewer* to number. "His troubles are less than mine" means "His troubles are not so great as mine." "His troubles are fewer than mine" means "His troubles are not so numerous as mine." It is, however, correct to say, "The signers of the petition were less than a hundred," where the round number "a hundred" is something like a collective noun, and "less" is thought of as meaning a less quantity or amount.

Like. Do not misuse for *as*. *Like* governs nouns and pronouns. Before phrases and clauses, *as* is the equivalent word.

✗ We spent the evening like in the old days.

☺ We spent the evening as in the old days.

✗ He thought like I did.

☺ He thought as I did (like me).

Line, along these lines. *Line* in the sense of *course of procedure, conduct, thought,* is allowable but has been so overworked, particularly in the phrase *along these lines*, that a writer who aims at freshness should discard it entirely.

✗ Mr. B. also spoke along the same lines.

☺ Mr. B. also spoke, to the same effect.

✗ He is studying along the line of modern art.

☺ He is studying modern art.

Literal, literally. Often incorrectly used in support of exaggeration or violent metaphor.

✗ A literal flood of abuse

☺ A flood of abuse

✗ Literally dead with fatigue

☺ Almost dead with fatigue (dead tired)

Lose out. Meant to be more emphatic than *lose*, but actually less so because of its commonness. The same holds true of *try out, win out, sign up.* With numerous verbs, *out* and *up* form idiomatic combinations: *find out, run out, cheer up, dry up, make up,* and others, each distinguishable in meaning from the simple verb. *Lose out* is not.

Most. Not to be used for *almost*.

  ✗ Most everybody

  ☺ Almost everybody

  ✗ Most all the time

  ☺ Almost all the time

Nature. Often simply redundant, used like *character*.

  ✗ Acts of a hostile nature

  ☺ Hostile acts

  ✗ He is by nature an optimistic person.

  ☺ He is an optimistic person.

Often vaguely used in such expressions as *lover of nature; poems about nature.* Unless more specific statements follow, the reader cannot tell whether the poems have to do with natural scenery, rural life, the sunset, the untracked wilderness, or the habits of squirrels.

Near by. Adverbial phrase, not yet fully accepted as good English, though the analogy of *close by* and *hard by* seems to justify it. *Near,* or *near at hand,* is as good, if not better.

Not to be used as an adjective; use *neighboring*.

Oftentimes, ofttimes. Archaic forms, no longer in good use. Substitute the word *often* instead.

One hundred and **one.** Retain the "and" in this and similar expressions.

One of the most. Avoid beginning essays or paragraphs with this construction, as, "One of the most interesting developments of modern science is," etc. "Switzerland is one of the most interesting countries of Europe." There is nothing wrong in this; it is simply threadbare and overused.

A common blunder is to use a singular verb in a relative clause following this or a similar expression, when the relative is the subject.

> ✗ One of the ablest men that has attacked this problem

> ☺ One of the ablest men that have attacked this problem

Participle for verbal noun. In the first sentences of the next two examples, *asking* and *accepting* are used as present participles; in the other examples, they are verbal nouns (gerunds). The construction shown in the first two sentences is occasionally found and has its defenders. Yet it is easy to see that the second pair of examples have to do not with a prospect of the Senate, but with a prospect of accepting. Here the construction is plainly illogical.

> ✗ Do you mind me asking a question?

> ☺ Do you mind my asking a question?

> ✗ There was no prospect of the Senate accepting even this compromise.

> ☺ There was no prospect of the Senate's accepting even this compromise.

As the authors of *The King's English* point out, there are sentences apparently, but not really, of this type, in which the possessive is not appropriate. For instance:

X I cannot imagine Lincoln refusing his assent to this measure.

In this sentence, what the writer cannot imagine is Lincoln himself, in the act of refusing his assent. Yet the meaning would be virtually the same, except for a slight loss of vividness, if he had written:

☺ I cannot imagine Lincoln's refusing his assent to this measure.

By using the possessive, the writer will always be on the safe side.

In the examples above, the subject of the action is a single, unmodified term immediately preceding the verbal noun, and the construction is as good as any that could be used. But any sentence in which the wording is clumsy, or in which the use of the possessive is awkward or impossible, should be recast.

X In the event of a reconsideration of the whole matter's becoming necessary

☺ If it should become necessary to reconsider the whole matter

X There was dissatisfaction with the decision of the arbitrators being favorable to the company.

☺ There was dissatisfaction that the arbitrators should have decided in favor of the company.

People. *The people* is a political term, not to be confused with *the public*. From the people comes political support or opposition; from the public comes artistic appreciation or commercial patronage.

Possess. Do not use this word as a substitute for *have* or *own*.

X He possessed great courage.

☺ He had great courage (was very brave).

✗ He was the fortunate possessor of

☺ He owned

Prove. The past participle is *proved*.

Respective, respectively. These words may usually be omitted from sentences without altering the meaning.

✗ Works of fiction are listed under the names of their respective authors.

☺ Works of fiction are listed under the names of their authors.

✗ The one-mile and two-mile runs were won by Jones and Cummings respectively.

☺ The one-mile and two-mile runs were won by Jones and by Cummings.

In some kinds of formal writing, as geometrical proofs, it may be appropriate to use *respectively*, but it should not appear in everyday writing.

Shall, Will. The future tense requires *shall* for the first person, will for the second and third. The formula to express the speaker's belief regarding his future action or state is *I shall*; *I will* expresses his determination or his consent.

➡ *Editor's Note:* With the exception of legal writing, *shall* is rarely used today. Chicago Style advises that it only be used to mean "has a duty to," and *shall not* is never used as the negative.

Should. See under *Would*.

So. Avoid, in writing, the use of *so* as an intensifier: *so good; so warm; so delightful*.

Sort of. See under *Kind of*.

Split Infinitive. There is precedent from the fourteenth century downward for interposing an adverb between *to* and the infinitive which it governs, but the construction is in disfavor and is avoided by nearly all careful writers.

✗ To diligently inquire

☺ To inquire diligently

➡ *Editor's Note:* Split infinitives are commonly found in both casual and formal writing today, and most contemporary style guides advise that such constructions are acceptable.

State. Should not be used as a mere substitute for *say* or *remark*. Restrict it to the sense of *express fully or clearly*, as, "He refused to state his objections."

Student Body. A needless and awkward expression meaning no more than the simple word *students*.

✗ A member of the student body

☺ A student

✗ Popular with the student body

☺ Liked by the students

✗ The student body assembled in the auditorium.

☺ The students assembled in the auditorium.

System. Often used without need; most of the time, such use is unnecessary and creates word clutter.

✗ Dayton has adopted the commission system of government.

☺ Dayton has adopted government by commission.

✗ The dormitory system

☺ Dormitories

Thanking You in Advance. This sounds as if the writer meant, "It will not be worth my while to write to you again." In making your request, write, "Will you please," or "I will appreciate," and if anything further seems necessary, write a letter of acknowledgment later.

They. A common grammatical error is the use of the plural pronoun when the antecedent is a distributive expression such as *each, each* one, *everybody, everyone, many a man*, which, though implying more than one person, requires the pronoun to be in the singular. Similar to this, but with even less justification, is the use of the plural pronoun with the antecedent *anybody, anyone, somebody, someone*, the intention being to avoid the awkward "he or she," or to avoid committing oneself to either. Some writers who are unsure of the correct construction will even write, "A friend of mine told me that they," etc.

Use *he* with all the above words, unless the antecedent is or must be feminine.

➡ *Editor's Note:* This grammar rule has changed over time. Today, the practice of writing *he* unless the feminine is indicated has fallen out of favor, replaced by other practices, including clumsy attempts at substitution. For a detailed discussion on gender in grammar, see *Elements of Style 2017*, Chapter 6 (Nouns—People, Places, Things), and Chapter 7 (Getting Personal With Pronouns).

Very. Use this word sparingly. Where emphasis is necessary, use strong words rather than relying on the overused *very*.

Viewpoint. Do not misuse this, as many do, for *view* or *opinion*. Instead, write *point of view*.

While. Avoid the indiscriminate use of this word in place of *and, but*, and *although*. Many writers use it frequently as a substitute for *and* or *but*, either from a desire to vary the connective or from uncertainty about which of the two connectives is the more appropriate. In this use, it is best replaced by a semicolon.

✗ The offices are on the ground floor, while the rest of the building is devoted to manufacturing.

☺ The offices are on the ground floor; the rest of the building is devoted to manufacturing.

Its use as a virtual equivalent of *although* is allowable in sentences where no ambiguity or absurdity is created.

☺ While I admire his energy, I wish it were employed in a better cause.

This is entirely correct, as shown by the paraphrase,

I admire his energy; at the same time, I wish it were employed in a better cause.

Compare:

✗ While the temperature reaches 95 degrees in the daytime, the nights are often chilly.

☺ Although the temperature reaches 95 degrees in the daytime, the nights are often chilly.

The paraphrase,

The temperature reaches 95 degrees in the daytime; at the same time the nights are often chilly,

shows why the use of *while* is incorrect.

In general, the writer will do well to use *while* only with strict literalness, in the sense of *during the time that*.

Whom. Often incorrectly used for *who* before *he said* or similar expressions, when it is really the subject of a following verb.

✗ His brother, whom he said would send him the money

☺ His brother, who he said would send him the money

✗ The man whom he thought was his friend

☺ The man who (that) he thought was his friend (whom he thought his friend)

Worthwhile. Overworked as a term of vague approval and (with *not*) of disapproval. Strictly applicable only to actions: "Is it worthwhile to study grammar?"

✗ His books are not worthwhile.

☺ His books are not worth reading (are not worth his while to read; are worthless).

The use of *worthwhile* before a noun ("a worthwhile story") is faulty grammar and should be avoided in writing.

Would. A conditional statement in first person requires *should*, not *would*.

I should not have succeeded without his help.

The equivalent of *shall* in indirect quotation after a verb in the past tense is *should*, not *would*.

He predicted that before long we should have a great surprise.

➡ *Editor's Note:* Because *shall* is less prevalent today, the rule calling for *should* to be used in conditional first-person statements may not apply, depending on the sentence and its intended meaning. For instance, if the writer wishes to convey that something ought to happen or should have happened, he might write, "She should have known better," and "She should have turned left at the intersection." Otherwise, *would* is often used today in conditional first-person statements.

To express habitual or repeated action, the past tense, without *would*, is usually sufficient, and from its brevity, more emphatic.

    X Once a year he would visit the old mansion.

    ☺ Once a year he visited the old mansion.

Chapter 6

SPELLING

The spelling of English words is not fixed and invariable, nor does it depend on any other authority than general agreement. In this day and age, agreement as to the spelling of most words is practically unanimous; but at any given moment, a relatively small number of words may be spelled in more than one way. As one of these forms comes to be generally preferred, the less customary form comes to look obsolete and is discarded. From time to time new forms, mostly simplifications, are introduced by innovators, and either win their place or die of neglect.

The practical objection to unaccepted and oversimplified spellings is the disfavor with which they are received by the reader. They distract his attention and exhaust his patience. He reads the form *though* automatically, without giving it a second thought; he reads the slang form *tho* and must mentally supply the missing letters, diverting a fraction of his attention from what is being read. The writer has defeated his own purpose.

➡ *Editor's Note:* This chapter in Strunk's first edition offered a list of sixty-five commonly misspelled words. The English language has expanded rapidly over the past century, and a plethora of new words have been introduced into everyday usage, causing writers headaches and typos. To offer some helpful guidance on frequently misspelled words, we have expanded the original list to the 171 words below.

WORDS OFTEN MISSPELLED

absence	acceptable
accidentally	accommodate

acquire	acquit
address	advice
affect	all right
amateur	apparent
arctic	argument
atheist	beginning
believe	bellwether
benefit	bicycle
broccoli	bureau
calendar	camaraderie
category	ceiling
cemetery	challenge
changeable	coarse
collectible	column
committed	conscience
conscientious	consensus
course	criticize
daiquiri	decease
deceive	definite
descent	describe
desperate	despise
develop	disappoint
disastrous	discipline
dissipate	drunkenness
duel	dumbbell
ecstasy	effect
embarrass	equipment

exercise	exhilarate
existence	experience
fascinate	fcbruary
fiery	fluorescent
foreign	formerly
gauge	grateful
guarantee	harass
height	hierarchy
humorous	hypocrisy
ignorance	immediate
immediately	impostor
incident	incidentally
independent	indispensable
inoculate	intelligence
jealous	jewelry
judgment	knowledge
latter	led
leisure	liaison
license	lose
maintenance	maneuver
marriage	mathematics
medieval	mediocre
memento	millennium
miniature	minuscule
miscellaneous	mischief
mischievous	misspell
murmur	mysterious

necessary	neighbor
noticeable	nuclear
occasion(ally)	occurred
occurrence	odyssey
opportunity	parallel
perseverance	personnel
piece	pigeon
playwright	possession
precede	preceding
prejudice	principal/principle
privilege	pronunciation
publicly	pursue
questionnaire	raspberry
receive	recommend
referred	repetition
restaurant	rhyme
rhythm	ridiculous
sacrilegious	schedule
scissors	seize
separate	sergeant
shepherd	siege
similar	simile
special	supersede
there/their/they're	thorough
threshold	through
tragedy	twelfth
tyranny	undoubtedly

vacuum	villain
weather	Wednesday
weird	

Note that a single consonant (other than *v*) preceded by a stressed short vowel is doubled before -*ed* and -*ing*, as in, *planned, letting, beginning;* but *coming* is an exception.

Write *to-day, to-night* and *to-morrow* (but not *together*) with a hyphen.

Write *any one, every one, some one, some time* (except in the sense of *formerly*) as two words.

➡ *Editor's Note:* The last two rules stated above are obsolete. It is now common practice to use the unhyphenated forms of *today, tonight* and *tomorrow,* and to omit, in most cases, the spaces from the pronouns *anyone, everyone, someone,* and *sometime.* In certain sentences, however, the two-word forms are still used. For example:

☺ Any one of those men could be the thief.

☺ I have read every one of Stephen King's books

Written as two words, *some time* denotes a passage of time. The following usages are correct:

☺ Some time has passed since we met.

☺ I will spend some time visiting you when I come to Ireland.

Chapter 7

STYLE RULES FOR BETTER WRITING

Much has changed in the English language since William Strunk wrote *Elements of Style* a century ago. Some of the grammar and style rules you probably learned in school have fallen out of favor. For instance, you may have been taught never to begin a sentence with "But" or "And." Never split an infinitive; and do not end a sentence with a preposition. In this chapter, we will look at whether these long-standing grammar rules still apply today, and we will review some essential style rules that modern writers should follow.

This chapter was not included in the first edition of Strunk's book. However, because an understanding of basic style rules is essential to coherent writing, we have included this excerpt from *Elements of Style 2017*, reprinted by permission. For an expanded handbook of modern grammar and style rules, see https://amazon.com/dp/B01MD0396I/.

Grammar is concerned with how words are used, and how words are combined into sentences and paragraphs. Style refers to an additional set of rules writers and editors should follow to achieve consistency in the construction and tone of their writing. Simply put, grammar rules will help you to write sentences that make sense, and style rules will help you to turn those sentences into a polished final draft.

Style is a term in writing that encompasses a wide variety of issues beyond grammar, such as questions on word usage, capitalization, how to abbreviate, how to write numbers and dates in running text, and many other quandaries. Style rules fill in the gray areas that exist because grammar rules tend to be broad. For instance, it might be possible to write a sentence in a dozen ways, and all might be grammatically correct; but one construction might be clearer and flow better than the rest. Style rules help to ensure that your writing expresses your ideas in the clearest and most effective manner possible.

Consider the following passage:

> Nine men stood by the wall, and 4 women stood next to the 2 cars. When the police approached, the crowd scattered, and three of the women jumped into 1 car and sped away.

This hodgepodge of digits and spelled-out numbers will be jarring and may seem unpolished to some readers. But if you follow a style rule that advises you, for instance, to spell out numbers up to 10 and writer higher numbers as digits, you will eliminate this sloppy syntax and achieve a better result, as in this revised passage:

> Nine men stood by the wall, and four women stood next to the two cars. When the police approached, the crowd scattered, and three of the women jumped into one car and sped away.

Dozens of writing style guides are available today. The most widely used, *Chicago Manual of Style,* is the bible of editors working in American English fiction genres, and some non-fiction editors. *AP Stylebook* is used by journalists and others who write and edit for news organizations and websites. *APA Style* and *MLA Style* are often used by college students for writing term papers and essays. In the United Kingdom, *Oxford Style Guide* is widely consulted for grammar questions.

Style guides are packed with rules on grammar, word usage, punctuation, and other writing technicalities. Some of these rules are rather complicated. A competent editor might devote six months to a year mastering all the intricacies of a particular style handbook. This investment of time, and the skill required to edit a manuscript cleanly and accurately, can be daunting for writers who wish to self-edit and produce a polished final draft. Some writers resort to hiring an editor; but good editors are in high demand and often charge substantial fees. Thus it is well worth a writer's time to study and follow whatever style primer he might need to use for academic or other writing endeavors .

Style guides sometimes give conflicting advice. For example, Chicago Style requires the use of serial commas, and AP Style advises against them. So, if you are editing by AP Style and use a serial comma, it's an error; but if you follow Chicago Style and don't use a serial comma, that is an error. To avoid confusion, you should follow the advice in your preferred style handbook and apply those rules consistently from the first page to the last of your manuscript.

To apply style effectively and elevate the quality of your writing, you should review a style guide from cover to cover, and take the time to familiarize yourself with its collection of rules. But the helpful pointers below will start you moving in the right direction.

You can start a sentence with a conjunction.

For more than century, grammarians have taught that you should never start a sentence with a coordinating conjunction. Seven of these conjunctions exist in English, and they are: *and, but, so, yet, or, for,* and *nor.* This prohibition may have developed out of grammar instructors wanting to help students avoid writing sentence fragments. But times have changed, and most style guides now advise that it is okay to start a sentence with a conjunction, as long as the practice is not overused.

The *Chicago Manual of Style* website advises: "No historical or grammatical foundation exists for considering sentences that begin with a conjunction to be in error." But the site also warns: "Sentences should begin with a conjunction only when the result is clear and more effective than some other alternative." The concern here is that starting too many sentences with conjunctions will give one's writing a choppy or singsong quality. Even dialogue, which is more forgiving, can bog down if so many sentences begin with conjunctions that readers take notice. Therefore, use this construction sparingly.

You can split infinitives.

An infinitive is a verb form that almost always begins with the word "to" and ends with a simple verb. For example: *to walk, to speak, to ask.* A split infinitive is a short phrase in which a word, typically an adverb, is inserted between the "to" and the verb, as, *to boldly go.*

For more than two hundred years, writers have been advised to avoid writing split infinitives. This edict is based on the notion that English derives from Latin, and it is not possible to split the infinitive of a verb in Latin because it is all one word. But English isn't Latin, and most style guides today advise that the rule against split infinitives is antiquated. *Chicago Manual of Style* states: "Sometimes it is perfectly appropriate to split an infinitive verb with an adverb to add emphasis or to produce a natural sound." Thus, it is no longer bad grammar to write the venerable phrase from *Star Trek*: "To boldly go where no man has gone before."

You can end a sentence with a preposition.

The rule against ending a sentence with a preposition goes back decades, but it now is obsolete. Chicago Style states: "The traditional caveat of yesteryear against ending sentences with prepositions is an unnecessary and pedantic restriction. The 'rule' prohibiting terminal prepositions was an ill-founded superstition."

Just because you can end a sentence with a preposition doesn't mean that you should. A sentence may read better if you eliminate the ending preposition and rewrite the sentence; or sometimes that preposition isn't even needed. Consider these sentences—the first ends with the preposition *at*, and the second reads better without it:

STYLE RULES FOR BETTER WRITING | 97

✗ Where are you at?

☺ Where are you?

A *phrasal verb* is a verb that consists of several words, and one word is always a preposition. Some examples of phrasal verbs include: *cheer up, drop out, log in.* It is always acceptable to end a sentence with a phrasal verb.

☺ I hope you *cheer up.*

☺ I love college, but I may have to *drop out.*

☺ Before you can read your email, you must *log in.*

Consider your audience.

Identify your intended audience before you start writing. Think about what your readers want to know about your topic, or what they will expect from your story that will make it an interesting or enjoyable read. Take into account their level of reading comprehension, the depth of their interest, and what is customary in your particular genre. Avoid the pitfall of "dumbing down" your writing to reach a wider audience. Focus on writing clearly and effectively so that your readers will grasp your thoughts and ideas or enjoy the story that you want to tell.

Write short paragraphs.

Generally, avoid writing long paragraphs, and especially avoid the convoluted and verbose styles commonly found in early twentieth-century literature. Large blocks of text are daunting to readers and suggest that what is to come will be boring or difficult to grasp. Shorter paragraphs are more inviting and easier to digest. Try to limit paragraphs to four or five sentences, or about 100-125 words.

A paragraph should discuss one main idea, not several. An idea might require twenty sentences to properly develop, but that doesn't mean that you should write a rambling, twenty-sentence paragraph that spans an entire page. Look for logical places where you can break a large block of text into several paragraphs.

In a long paragraph, you typically will have at least one or two transitional terms. For example, a sentence might start with a word or phrase as *Next, Furthermore, In addition,* or *However.* You can break a paragraph at this point and allow the next paragraph to begin with one of these transitions. Just make sure that the smaller paragraphs are unified in themselves.

Write concise sentences.

For the same reason that you should avoid writing lengthy paragraphs, you should write crisp, concise sentences that are easy to read and follow. Verbose sentence constructions were common in the past; but readers today process information more readily when it is presented in small chunks. Consider the two examples below: the first is verbose, the second is clear and concise. You can probably guess which construction most readers would prefer:

✗ In light of the fact that the report does not include specific examples in its discussion of ways to improve workplace safety, we are of the strong belief that it should undergo revision.

☺ We believe the report should be revised because it does not include examples of how to improve workplace safety.

Be consistent with style.

Good writing is built on patterns of words and sentences, so whether you are writing a news story, a press release, a spicy love story, or a technical manual, you should follow style rules and be consistent in their application. Avoid switching back and forth from digits to spelled-out numbers; for instance, by writing "ten pens" in one sentence and "10 pencils" in the next. Don't refer to an iPhone in one sentence, call it a cell phone in the next, and call it a mobile device on the next page. Some writers do this deliberately in the belief that it adds interest to their prose, but it merely confuses readers and muddles what they are trying to say. Readers will notice these vacillations and be distracted trying to figure out the writer's reason for switching back and forth.

Write with a word, not with a phrase.

Word clutter is a serious problem in nearly every form of writing. Using extra words unnecessarily can make the task of reading confusing and tedious. Trim phrases that consist of multiple words when a single word works just as well.

> ✗ *As a matter of fact*, I'm having second thoughts *at this point in time.*

> ☺ In fact, I'm having second thoughts now.

> ➡ Even better: "I'm having second thoughts now."

> ✗ *During the period* I was in Mexico, *there is no doubt but that* I had a great time.

> ☺ While I was in Mexico, I had a great time.

Don't double up terms.

Some inexperienced writers will place two words with the same or very similar meanings next to one another in a sentence. These "double terms" are redundant and add word clutter. If you notice a duplicated word or phrase in your writing and you can delete it without changing the meaning of the sentence, then you should remove it.

> ✗ This fruit must be *washed* and *cleaned.*

> ➡ *Washed* and *cleaned* mean the same, so use one word or the other.

> ✗ The deeds must be *entered* and *recorded.*

> ➡ *Entered* and *recorded* mean the same, so use one or word the other.

✗ The program will *begin* and *commence*...

☺ The program will *start*...

✗ *The measure and breadth* of the problem...

☺ *The scope* of the problem...

Place modifiers next to the word modified.

Modifiers should be placed next to the word they modify whenever possible. If several expressions modify the same word, write the sentence so that no ambiguity or incorrect relationship is suggested.

✗ *All the teachers* were *not* present.

☺ Not all the teachers were present.

✗ While walking in the park, Connie found a *silver* woman's *wedding ring*.

☺ While walking in the park, Connie found a woman's *silver wedding ring*.

✗ He *only* found *two typos* in the book.

☺ He found *only two typos* in the book.

In the example below, the first passage is rewritten to follow this rule, improving the flow of the sentence.

✗ Jack Jones will give a lecture on Tuesday evening, to which the public is invited, on "Global Trade" at 8 p.m.

☺ On Tuesday evening at 8 p.m., Jack Jones will give a lecture on "Global Trade." The public is invited.

Place long conditions after the main clause.

Long or wordy conditions (such as the italicized words in the example below) should be placed after the main clause to improve clarity. In this way, you focus the reader's attention on the major idea you are stating in the sentence, and then you explain the condition.

✗ *If you own more than fifty acres and cultivate grapes*, you are subject to water rationing.

☺ You are subject to water rationing *if you own more than 50 acres and cultivate grapes.*

Avoid intruding words.

"Intruders" are another type of word clutter and contribute nothing to the meaning of a sentence. Common intruders include the words: *program, method, event, effort, conditions,* and *activities.* In the examples below, the intruding words are underlined. Notice that removing these words does not change the meaning of the sentences and, in fact, improves the flow.

✗ Library books and paper records are endangered by fluctuating temperature <u>conditions.</u>

☺ Library books and paper records are endangered by fluctuating temperatures.

✗ The new policy simplifies reporting <u>activities</u>.

☺ The new policy simplifies reporting.

✗ The cataloging <u>effort</u> is proceeding on schedule.

☺ The cataloging is proceeding on schedule.

A person is a *who*, not a *that*.

Use *who* with the pronouns *he* and *she*, and with nouns that refer to people. Use *that* with objects.

✗ He is the person *that* came to the meeting.

☺ He is the person *who* came to the meeting.

➡ (Many writers make this mistake.)

✗ This is the couch *who* I just bought.

☺ This is the couch *that* I just bought.

➡ (Very few writers make this mistake!)

Which and *that* are not interchangeable.

Contrary to the popular notion, *which* is not a more elegant way to say *that*. The two words are not interchangeable, and the choice is not a matter of style—following this rule is a right-or-wrong choice.

Which is a pronoun that introduces nonessential information. Use a comma before a *which* clause. If a comma won't work, then you should be using *that*.

➡ If you delete the words in a *which* clause, the remaining words should still form a full sentence.

That is a pronoun used to introduce essential information. Do not use a comma before *that*.

✗ Cars *which* burn fossil fuels emit pollutants.

☺ Cars *that* burn fossil fuels emit pollutants.

✗ Cars *that* are one form of transportation may emit pollutants.

☺ Cars, *which* are one form of transportation, may emit pollutants.

So, if you can use the word *that*, use it. If you don't have a comma before the word *which*, use *that*. If you delete the words in the *which* clause and the sentence does not make sense, use *that*.

Often, *that* can be omitted.

Using the word *that* in a sentence is often not necessary. It is not wrong to include the extra word in most cases, but modern style guides suggest omitting *that* when you can do so without affecting the clarity of the sentence.

☺ The lunch *that* I ate yesterday was good.

Preferred: The lunch I ate yesterday was good.

☺ The cars *that* were sold in 2015 have better brakes.

Preferred: The cars sold in 2015 have better brakes.

Generally, you should include *that* after verbs implying assertion or speaking, such as: advise, advocate, agree, assert, assume, calculate, conceive, claim, content, declare, estimate, hold, imagine, insist, learn, maintain, make clear, point out, propose, state, and suggest.

☺ I *assume that* you passed your English test.

✗ I *assume* you passed your English test.

☺ He couldn't *imagine that* his wife would leave.

✗ He couldn't *imagine* his wife would leave.

☺ Joe *insists that* he knows everything.

✗ Joe *insists* he knows everything.

Include *that* before clauses beginning with conjunctions, such as *after, although, since,* and *so.*

Avoid *this is because, that is the result of.*

Do not begin sentences with *This is because, That is because, That is a result of, It is due to,* or similar phrases. These constructions are ambiguous and confusing. Repeat the subject from the previous sentence, even if it requires more words to complete the sentence.

✗ The sales tax will increase on May 1. *This is because of* the new law.

☺ The sales tax will increase on May 1. *This higher tax is because of* the new law.

☺ Even better: The sales tax will increase on May 1 because of the new law.

✗ The power plant generated more electricity in July. *It was due to* the weather.

☺ The power plant generated more electricity in July. *The increased demand was due to* the weather.

☺ Even better: The power plant generated more electricity in July due to the weather.

Make sure subjects and verbs agree.

Singular nouns take singular verbs, and plural nouns take plural verbs. This advice sounds straightforward enough, but it can be confusing with collective nouns such as *staff* and *family*, and when plural words are added between the subject and the verb.

✗ The <u>author</u> of the books and articles <u>are</u>...

☺ The <u>author</u> of the books and articles <u>is</u>...

✗ The import <u>level</u> of corn and wheat <u>are</u>...

☺ The import <u>level</u> of corn and wheat <u>is</u>...

✗ Our <u>success</u> in marketing books <u>make</u> us...

☺ Our <u>success</u> in marketing books <u>makes</u> us...

✗ Our <u>forecast</u>, together with the computer models, <u>show</u> that...

☺ Our <u>forecast</u>, together with the computer models, <u>shows</u> that...

Avoid confusing adjectives and adverbs.

Adjectives and adverbs are closely related in their forms and use, but do not confuse the two. When you want to modify a noun or pronoun, use an adjective. When you want to modify a verb, an adjective, or an adverb, use an adverb.

George smells *bad.*

➡ *Bad* is an adjective describing *George*; that is, George needs a bath.

George smells *badly.*

➡ *Badly* is an adverb describing *smells*; that is, George's nose does not work well.

I feel *poor.*

➡ *Poor* is an adjective describing *I*; that is, I'm ill or out of money.

I have a headache and feel *poorly.*

➡ *Poorly* is an adverb describing *feel*; that is, my sense of touch is not very good.

To avoid confusing adjectives and adverbs, consider the modifier you intend to use. If you want to write that Ellen says things that are foolish, identify the adjective and adverb forms: *foolish* is an adjective and can only modify a noun or pronoun, while *foolishly* is an adverb and can only modify a verb, an adjective, or another adverb.

✗ She talks *foolish.* (The adjective *foolish* can only modify the pronoun *She.*)

☺ She is *foolish.* (The adjective *foolish* modifies the pronoun *She.*)

☺ She talks *foolishly.* (The adverb *foolishly* modifies the verb *talks.*)

If you want to use the adjective *foolish* in the sentence, you must add either a noun or a pronoun. For example, add the noun *things* and then you could write:

☺ She says *foolish* things.

Avoid the false subjects *it is, there is/are,* etc.

The term "false subjects" refers to phrases such as: *it is, it was, it will be, there is, there are, there was, there were,* and *there will be.* They usually occur at the beginning of a sentence and often displace the real subject. This is a lazy habit, and it can cause ambiguity and awkward syntax. In nearly every instance, a sentence that starts with a false subject can be rewritten for an improved and grammatically correct result. The examples below list some of the false subjects you should avoid and give suggested replacements.

✗ It is revealed in the video

☺ The video reveals

✗ It was claimed by the prosecutor

☺ The prosecutor claimed

✗ There are times when

☺ Sometimes (or Occasionally)

✗ It will be announced by the candidate

☺ The candidate will announce

✗ There were failures because of

☺ Failures were caused by

✗ There will be protests unless

☺ Protests will occur unless

Chapter 8

STUDY GUIDE

The original *Elements of Style* was written a century ago by William Strunk Jr., an English professor at Cornell University. Over the years, it has been reprinted in numerous editions, and today, it is widely recognized as a classic. Some of the grammar rules in the book are antiquated; nevertheless, it is required reading for many college students taking literature and other writing classes.

This version of *Elements of Style: Classic Edition (2018 Update)*, remains true to Prof. Strunk's original work, and it contains all the material published in the first edition, as well as a new, expanded Foreword on the importance of having a fundamental grasp of English grammar, and two new chapters:

Basic Rules of Capitalization (Chapter 3) provides an extensive collection of capitalization rules, addressing points of confusion for many writers; and,

Style Rules for Better Writing (Chapter 7) offers useful tips on how to improve one's writing, and frequent style mistakes to avoid when revising and self-editing.

Front Matter

The Preface contains introductory remarks about the purpose of the book, which is to serve as a quick crash course for those seeking to master the fundamentals of English Grammar. It goes on to summarize revisions and additions made by the editor to the Classic Edition and to this 2018 Update.

In the Foreword, *Why English Grammar Matters*, the importance of writing clearly and correctly, and the paramount role of grammar in the writing process, are examined. This section offers a briefly overview of the nine parts of speech; three essentials of effective writing; and practical advice for students and writers from author George Orwell.

Chapter 1

In *Elementary Rules of Usage*, Prof. Strunk's first seven rules of English Grammar are presented:

Rule 1 offers guidelines on how to form the possessive singular of nouns by adding 's, and exceptions to this rule.

Rule 2 examines how to correctly punctuate (with commas) sentences having three or more elements and a single conjunction. An editor's note included here advises that this particular method of punctuation makes use of what is called the serial comma, or Oxford comma.

Rule 3 focuses on the rules for enclosing parenthetic expressions between commas.

Rule 4 is another comma-related guideline calling for this punctuation mark to be placed before a conjunction that introduces a coordinate clause.

Rule 5 cautions the writer against using a comma to join independent clauses.

Rule 6 explains that sentences should not be split in two meaning do not use periods where commas should be used. Strunk gives examples of how this can create unacceptable sentence fragments.

Rule 7 advises that a participial phrase at the beginning of a sentence must refer to the grammatical subject. Examples are given to show how this rule should be applied.

Chapter 2

Elementary Principles of Composition presents additional grammar rules, beginning with Rule 8, which focuses on the importance of the paragraph as the principal unit of composition. Rule 9 points out that each paragraph must begin with a topic sentence, and several pages of discussion follow, with examples of how to develop paragraphs for a typical academic composition.

Rule 10 covers active voice and why it is often advisable to use it. Some instances where use of the passive voice is appropriate are mentioned.

Rule 11 examines the importance of putting statements in positive form, which allows the writer to make definite, forceful assertions. Examples are given showing how overuse of the word *not* can lead to weak and indecisive writing.

Rule 12 builds on the previous rules, exploring the advantages of using definite, concrete language. Nearly three pages are devoted to this crucial topic.

Rule 13 explains that vigorous writing is concise. The writer must endeavor to omit needless words from sentences, and unnecessary sentences from paragraphs. This rule examines the problem of "word clutter" and what to do about it.

Rule 14 offers guidance on how to achieve concise, crisp writing by avoiding loose structures that can become monotonous to readers. Strunk explains that one fix for this is to avoid repetitive use of connectives such as *and, but,* and *so.*

Rule 15 explores the principle of parallel construction and gives examples of preferred writing styles, and sentence structures to be avoided.

Rule 16 explains that related words should be kept together to avoid interrupting the flow of the main clause. Strunk examines how the subject of a sentence and its verb should not be separated by a phrase or clause that can written at the beginning of the sentence with better effect. He also explains how this rule applies to nouns, pronouns, and modifiers.

Rule 17 admonishes the writer to avoid changing tenses when summarizing actions or facts. Examples are given that show how violating this rule can lead to stilted or ambiguous writing.

Rule 18, the last rule in this chapter, explains that the emphatic words of a sentence should be placed at the end of the sentence for maximum effect.

Chapter 3

Basic Rules of Capitalization provides a series of fifteen in-depth rules covering capitalization, including "first word" capitalization; proper nouns, days, months, historic eras, and the names of seasons; when to capitalize landmarks, religious titles, political titles, job and education titles; and other essential rules every student and writer should know. This is new material that did not appear in Strunk's original *Elements of Style* or the first release of this Classic Edition in 2017.

Chapter 4

A Few Matters of Form gives brief advice on how to write headings, numerals, references, and titles. Hyphenation is briefly mentioned as well. An editor's note appears here to alert readers to the fact that hyphenation rules have changed over the years, and some updated rules are given.

This chapter also discusses how to handle parentheses and quotations in typical sentences. These sections are brief and provide only cursory insights into these topics.

Chapter 5

Words and Expressions Often Misused presents an alpha-betized list that begins with an entry for *alright*, which Prof. Strunk advises is not a word and should never appear in edited writing. It concludes with entries on the always vexing *Whom*, the overused word *worthwhile*, and advice on the use of *would* versus *should*. This final rule includes an editor's note discussing present-day usage of these words. Strunk's admonition to avoid split infinitives is addressed in a separate editor's note stating that split infinitives are acceptable today in most forms of writing.

Chapter 6

This chapter presents a list of frequently misspelled words in the English language. Strunk's original edition of *Elements of Style* featured sixty-five words. The list in this Classic Edition has been expanded to 171 words that often cause headaches for students and writers.

Chapter 7

This chapter on *Style Rules for Better Writing* opens with an explanation of why writers should follow style rules, and how such rules can help them to produce concise and well written manuscripts. The chapter presents 19 up-to-date style rules, with examples, on topics ranging from starting a sentence with a conjunction to splitting infinitives and ending a sentence with a preposition. The chapter explores the practical benefit of writing short paragraphs and concise sentences; placing modifiers next to the words modified; why intruding words should be avoided, and other style-related topics. This chapter, like Chapter 3, is new and has not appeared in previous editions of this book.

Chapter 8

This study guide—it does not appear in Strunk's original *Elements of Style* and has been added by the editor to give a brief overview of the topics covered in this book, which may be helpful to students for whom this book is required reading.

-#-

Elements of Style 2017
Edited by Richard De A'Morelli

This essential handbook for writers presents a collection of grammar, style, and punctuation rules to help you to write well, self-edit efficiently, and produce a grammar-perfect final draft. It is a major update to William Strunk's 1921 grammar classic. Much has changed in the world since then—some of the rules in Strunk's book are obsolete, and new grammar and style rules have come into play that writers must know.

Bestselling author/editor Richard De A'Morelli shares his 30+ years of experience as a senior editor, explaining what every writer should know about modern grammar and style. Written in plain English, with easy-to-follow examples, this book takes the headache out of great writing. Read any chapter, follow the practical advice, and you will see an over-night improvement in your writing. Read a chapter a day, and in just a few weeks, you will be amazed by the polished quality of your final draft.

If you write anything at all for work, school, or your own enjoyment, you should have a copy of this writer's handbook on your desk.

Buy online at http://spectrum.org/books/elements

ISBN Numbers	Editions
978-1-988236-26-1	MOBI/Kindle
978-1-988236-28-5	Paperback
978-1-088236-31-5	Paperback Large Print

Notes

Notes

Notes

Notes

Made in the USA
Coppell, TX
30 July 2020